RAPE AND RITUAL

Marie-Louise von Franz, Honorary Patron

**Studies in Jungian Psychology
by Jungian Analysts**

Daryl Sharp, General Editor

RAPE AND RITUAL

A Psychological Study

Bradley A. Te Paske

For Maurice A. Te Paske, 1917-1976.

Canadian Cataloguing in Publication Data

Te Paske, Bradley A. (Bradley Alan), 1951-
   Rape and ritual

(Studies in Jungian psychology by Jungian analysts; 10)
Bibliography: p.
Includes index.
ISBN 0-919123-09-0

1. Rape—Psychological aspects. 2. Rape—
Mythology. 3. Jung, C. G. (Carl Gustav), 1875-1961.
I. Title. II. Series: Studies in Jungian
psychology; 10.

RC560.R36T36   364.1′532′019   C82-094883-7

INNER CITY BOOKS
Box 1271, Station Q, Toronto, Canada M4T 2P4
Telephone (416) 484-4562

Honorary Patron: Marie-Louise von Franz.
Publisher and General Editor: Daryl Sharp.
Editorial Board: Fraser Boa, Daryl Sharp, Marion Woodman.

INNER CITY BOOKS was founded in 1980 to promote the
understanding and practical application of the work of C.G. Jung.

Cover: Roman abducting a Sabine woman, 16th-century engraving by
Jan Mueller.—From *The Illustrated Bartsch*, vol. 4, Abaris Books,
New York, 1980.

Glossary and Index by Daryl Sharp.

Illustrations selected by the author and the editor.

Printed and bound in Canada by Webcom Limited

CONTENTS

See last pages for descriptions of other INNER CITY BOOKS

Preface

I am sitting in a street cafe in Naples talking with a gracious old Catholic sister. Behind her I see a very appealing whore in the street.

With my father and a friend in the capital city: We are going to meet a very important politician, but first must meet my father's political cohorts. I feel more or less shoved around in the proceedings. Entering the hotel lobby to meet the illustrious politician, I see it has suddenly been transformed into a hospital emergency room. Policemen stand around. A cheap magazine there carries reports of a young woman who has been raped and murdered.

Suddenly I stand alone in this emergency room with two women. The first is nearly dead. She has been terribly beaten, has deep cuts on her head and a couple of fingers torn off. She sighs breathlessly, "Just one more shot, just one more shot..." and I think, "*Gnadenschuss?*" [mercy killing]. The second woman is a nurse who is very soberly and quietly caring for the suffering young girl. It is so tragic that I am deeply moved and nearly crying. But then my father is there —he tells me that a dying aunt collects three million francs a month on interest alone.

Then I am very high up in the mountains. I see there an old Greek up even higher in a mysterious place where columns of red sandstone stand before caves and passageways. There is a view out over a vast expanse of land. (It reminds me of Christ being tempted by the Devil in a movie I saw.) The Greek man gives forth with deeply heartfelt and imploring cries. Again and again the strong anguished voice echoes in the rocks: "Why, why can there be no peace!" He has—as I simultaneously realize I have—a great fantasy of a square temple high atop a rocky mountain. (It might be the temple of Aphaea on Aegina.)

The above dream reflects the painfully ironic and tense psychic atmosphere in which a psychological work invariably begins. This study of rape, ritual and psychological development unquestionably shares that pang of emotion in the hospital room, and likewise shall be unable to conceal an ultimate fervor for the Greek man's ideal. But unfortunately, as the dream so sorely demonstrates, sympathy and transcendence are just not enough.

In confronting so pressing and ubiquitous a contemporary problem as rape, a credo of "Get thee behind me, Satan" constitutes a fundamental betrayal of woman and of the future self a man might one day know. The present study begins then with shadow, remains close to earth, is preoccupied with a black and serpentine Eros. However, through turning around and reflecting upon its fierce pursuit, by lighting a lamp here or dropping an ax there, we may come to a sense of the transformation of the instinct.

7

In what follows, the reader is invited to consider each angle of approach to the problem of rape with the individual personality in mind: the individual meeting the problem in the newspaper, through reading feminist or psychological literature, by personally knowing, or even becoming, a victim of sexual assault, and finally, as one discovering the involvement of his or her own psyche in the sexual violence of our time. Only by beginning with the mundane facts of criminal rape will the way be adequately paved to a consideration of the role of the Great Mother, the archetype of the masculine, of anima and Eros, ego and shadow, and finally of sacrifice in the psychology of rape.

Athenian youths in pursuit.—Terracotta amphora, Attica, 6th century B.C. (Metropolitan Museum of Art).

1

The Crime of Rape

A Problem for Men

Since the phenomenology of rape appears on a broad spectrum, it is imperative to begin with the mundane reality of rape as a criminal act. What sort of crime is rape, by whom is it committed and who falls victim to this particular form of assault?

In the United States the "Big Four" violent crimes are murder, assault, rape and armed robbery. The number of rapes increased throughout the seventies in proportion to the rise in other crimes. In the year 1973, for example, there were 51,000 "founded" cases of rape or attempted rape in the United States, whereas in 1980 more than 82,000 came to the attention of law enforcement officials.[1] ("Founded" refers only to those cases reported in which intercourse was achieved and confirmed by police or medical personnel.) Taking even the very conservative rule-of-thumb of five rapes for every one reported to the police, this means an increase from 255,000 to as many as 400,000 cases per year.

"When other crimes of violence are compared statistically with rape," notes Susan Brownmiller in *Against Our Will,* "the profile of the forcible rapist falls at a point midway between the profile of the man who commits aggravated assault and the man who commits robbery."[2] This is significant, for as she further points out:

> Like assault, rape is an act of physical damage to another person, and like robbery it is also an act of acquiring property: the intent is to "have" the female body in the acquisitory meaning of the term. A woman is perceived by the rapist as both hated person and desired property. Hostility *against* her and possession *of* her may be simultaneous motivations; and the hatred is expressed in the same act that is the attempt to "take" her against her will. In one violent crime, rape is an act against person and property.[3]

The violence of a crime occurring with such frequency presses upon us—particularly upon men—the responsibility of taking the problem of rape very seriously, though excuses for not doing so abound. Not long ago, in 1900, even the leading authority on sexuality and its perversions, Richard Krafft-Ebing, could maintain the moralistic assumption that "it is highly improbable that a man morally intact would commit this most brutal crime,"[4] or again aid his generation of psychologists in evading a confrontation with the

9

problem of rape by simply projecting the whole problem onto the village idiot: "It is a fact that rape is very often the act of degenerate male imbeciles, who under some circumstances do not even respect the bond of blood."[5] Krafft-Ebing devotes a mere seven of 600 pages to the rape problem and discusses only three rapists—an idiot, a moral imbecile and a weak-minded epileptic! His minimal treatment of rape amounts to little more than an official sloughing off of the whole problem. A significant correlate of this tendency is Krafft-Ebing's general attitude toward women. So pressed is he to show the position of the European woman in a positive light that he compares her to the women of Islam:

> Above all things Islamism excludes women from public life and enterprise, and stifles her intellectual and moral advancement. The Mohammedan woman is simply a means for sensual gratification and the propagation of the species; whilst in the sunny balm of Christian doctrine, blossom forth her divine virtues and her qualities of housewife, companion and mother. What a contrast![6]

Grand illusion—but only one of many before and since which, along with many more calculated misogynist positions, men have embraced in order to elude the problem of rape.

The Freudian attitude, influential in psychiatry and criminology, has been as responsible as any popular notions for propagating the stereotype of the rapist as some extraordinary sexual deviant—the mild-mannered, sexually repressed psychopath dominated by women who one day goes crazy and rapes in an uncontrollable passion. Speaking of just this conception of the rapist, the sociologist Diana E.H. Russell points out:

> One function of the myth that rape is only perpetrated by society's freaks is that rape then appears to have no further implications for the rest of society. All the sane men must protect "their" women from the few insane ones, a woman without men must watch out. Yet rape is *not* exclusively the act of sadistic psychopaths and is much more widespread than most people realize. Indeed, the view emerges ... that rape is not so much a deviant act as an over-conforming act.[7]

At least it springs from a set of sexist attitudes which many men share.

While there has been the occasional dabbling by psychologists into the motivations and psychodynamics of rapists, it has been sociologists and criminologists who have given us the bare facts of the matter. One might ask just how the crime of rape amounts to an "over-conforming act"? The pioneer work *Patterns in Forcible Rape*, by Menachem Amir, answers the question. Brownmiller reports that the single most important contribution of Amir's Philadelphia study was to place the rapist squarely within the subculture of violence.

The rapist, it was revealed, "has no separate identifiable pathology aside from the individual quirks and personality disturbances that might characterize any single offender who commits any sort of crime."[8] Amir discovered that in sharp contrast to the myth of "uncontrollable lust," the act of rape is "usually planned in advance and elaborately arranged by a single rapist or a group of buddies."[9] Amir expressed his surprise at the fact that one-half (though statistics vary) of the rapes occurring in the United States involve two or more assailants, and also that "psychiatric literature on rape had treated the phenomenon of group rape with silence."[10] The United States *Uniform Crime Reports* for the year 1973 show statistically that 61 percent of rapists are under the age of 25; the largest concentration is in the 16 to 24 age range. According to the FBI, 47 percent are black, 51 percent are white, and "all other races" comprise the remainder.[11] These percentages were generally the same in the 1980 *Uniform Crime Reports*.

To a high degree rape is a crime which correlates statistically with social deprivation. Criminologist Marvin Wolfgang, Amir's mentor at the University of Pennsylvania's school of criminology, remarks that "social class... looms large in all studies of violent crime."[12] Wolfgang's theory of the "subculture of violence" described by Brownmiller is as follows:

> Within the dominant value system of our culture there exists a subculture formed of those from the lower classes, the poor, the disenfranchised, the black, whose values often run counter to those of the dominant culture, the people in charge. The dominant culture can operate within the laws of civility because it has little need to resort to violence to get what it wants. The subculture, thwarted, inarticulate and angry, is quick to resort to violence; indeed, violence and physical aggression become a common way of life, particularly for young males.[13]

Some idea may be gained here about the sociology of rape as a violent crime occurring in and perpetuated by an overtly violent segment of society. But rape has its subtler forms as well, and before churning up fear and loathing for the sexual violence of oppressed classes, one may pause to question whether or not the American businessman's "extra pillow" at the freeway motel or the European tourist's liaison with some local girl in Bangkok constitutes operating "within the laws of civility."

Rapists include husbands—albeit that by legal definition wives in most states cannot be raped by their husbands—as well as lovers; one 1953 study at Indiana University showed that the ten worst cases of the 6.2 percent of women who had suffered forceful attempts at sexual intercourse, including verbal threats and physical pain, were dating regularly, pinned or engaged.[14] Psychotherapists are by no means excluded from the list of sexual offenders. A paper entitled "Dealing therapeutically with women who have been involved with their psychotherapists," distributed by the Walk-In Counseling Center of Minneapolis, indicates how extensive this problem may be:

> A study by Kardener, Fuller, and Mensh (1973) reported that of a sample of psychiatrists who responded to their survey, 10% reported having engaged in erotic behavior with clients (5% to the point of intercourse). Grunebaum, Nadelson, and Macht (1976) found that 50% of the psychiatrists in their sample knew of specific instances of sexual involvement between client and therapist, even though most had not reported this to any official body of the profession. Sexual exploitation of clients has also been reported with gay clients (Schoener, 1976), with women in treatment for drug abuse problems (Ponsor, Soler, Abod, 1976), by paraprofessional counselors working for a hotline (Schoener, 1974). Victims even include young professionals in training (APA Report on the Task Force on Sex Bias and Sex-Role Stereotyping, 1975). One dissertation (Belote, 1974) contains reports on 25 cases and we know of one in preparation which is expected to report on an even larger sample. An ever-growing literature not to mention occasional lawsuits further testifies to the existence of the problem.[15]

In instances such as these—many doubtless far from the legal definition of rape, and some crossing an indistinct line toward less serious seduction—a subtle influence is at work, namely the prestige and power of the individual in his professional role. Far from being limited to the mentally deficient, the violent criminal, lower classes or blacks, and groups of witless buddies, the problem of rape extends even to the psychologist's consulting room where it must be confronted not only by him, but *within* him.

It is perhaps naively assumed that the reader does not blame women. Ever since Eve and Pandora the responsibility for sexual evil has been projected onto woman. Today the responsibility for rape is being rightfully returned to men, to be grappled with by those courageous enough to look inside themselves and magnanimous enough to seriously consider what feminists have to say on the subject. The topic of rape is a hot coal placed in the hand. With the exception of male-on-male rapes, which occur almost exclusively in prison settings, and the very rare sexual assault of men by women, rape is a sexist crime against women.

The general background of rape—the social, physiological and emotional differences between the sexes—is exhaustively and exhaustingly discussed in Simone de Beauvoir's *The Second Sex* (1949). Her specific references to rape, however, are few. Influenced as she is by Helene Deutsch and Freud, her attention centers on the erotic anxieties of adolescent girls. Similarly, though elaborately critical of the social position of women, neither Betty Friedan's *The Feminine Mystique* (1963) nor Germaine Greer's *The Female Eunuch* (1971) deals with rape specifically. Not until 1973 were the history, politics and social phenomenology of rape elaborated in the meticulously researched and important book *Against Our Will: Men, Women and Rape* by Susan Brownmiller. Brownmiller's work has been the most important single source of the present study. She brings attention to bear on a sizeable body of historical material, traditional myths and psychological theories about rape, all of which she scrutinizes as the evidence and elaboration of male chauvinism.

Brownmiller claims that the earliest examples of this male chauvinism are found in the ancient legal codes. Ancient Hebrew law, for example, viewed rape "as a property crime of man against man. Woman was of course viewed as property."[16] "Criminal rape, as a patriarchal father saw it, was a violation of the new way of doing business. It was, in a phrase, the theft of virginity, an embezzlement of his daughter's fair price on the market."[17] She refers here of course to the dowry systems of ancient Babylon and Israel. Among the Assyrians, "the father of a raped virgin was permitted to seize the wife of the rapist and violate her in turn."[18] Under the Code of Hammurabi a woman was "either a betrothed virgin, living in the house of her father, or else she was somebody's lawfully wedded wife and lived in the house of her husband."[19] Reflecting the fear for the protection of pristine goods, the man raping a betrothed virgin would be executed, whereas a "married woman who had the misfortune to get raped in Babylon had to share the blame equally with her attacker. Regardless of how the incident occurred, the crime was labelled adultery and both participants were bound and thrown into the river."[20]

Not until 13th-century England was the legal concept of criminal rape "broadened by the manorial courts to include at least in principle the rape of 'matrons, nuns, widows, concubines and even prostitutes.'"[21] Banned about the same time was the curious custom of allowing rapists to redeem themselves—if not their victims—by marriage. Most convincingly Brownmiller illuminates the proprietary attitude of men toward women in history, the sort we have already seen in Krafft-Ebing, and the snail's pace at which legislation recognizing women's rights has crept along. One small contemporary step forward was the 1978 court case in Oregon in which suit was brought against a husband for rape. More recently, rape and assault charges were brought against a husband in France whose new bride was not only forcibly taken but received 14 knife wounds before being abandoned in a park.

Under the relatively stable conditions in a kingdom or modern state, some form of justice is meted out despite certain sexist elements marring the system. In times of upheaval, however, as in war, women like so many plots of land become with renewed clarity the disputed possessions of men, their bodies an inevitable part of the battleground. As Brownmiller observes:

> Down through the ages, triumph over women by rape became a way to measure victory, part of a soldier's proof of masculinity and success, a tangible reward for services rendered.[22]

And again, on the side of the defeated army:

> Men of a conquered nation traditionally view the rape of "their women" as the ultimate humiliation, a sexual *coup de grace*. Rape is considered by the people of a defeated nation to be a part of the enemy's conscious effort to destroy them. In fact, by tradition, men appropriate the rape of "their women" as part of their own male anguish of defeat. This egocentric view does have partial validity. Apart from a genuine, human concern for wives and daughters near and dear to them, rape by a conqueror *is* compelling evidence of the conquered's status of masculine impotence.[23]

Of the systematic employment of rape as a method of terror in war, Brownmiller cites a number of examples. Perhaps most impressive are the 1947 "Rape of Nanking" where invading Japanese perpetrated an estimated 20,000 rapes within the first month of their occupation of that city, and the sexual violence of the 1971 Bangladesh war of independence where Pakistani troops reportedly raped anywhere from 200,000 to 400,000 Bengali women. Similar tactics have been employed by Germans against Jews and Russians, reciprocally by Russian troops during the counterinvasion of eastern Germany and, along with many others, by American men in Vietnam. A pointed sense of dread grips one upon reading the interviews with American Vietnam veterans who finally dared to speak of sexual violence:

> "They only do it when there are lots of guys around," veteran George Phillips told writer Lucy Komisar. "You know, it makes them feel good. They show each other what they can do—'I can do it,' you know. They won't do it by themselves."
> "Did you rape too?"
> "Nope."
> "Why not?"
> "I don't know, I just got a thing. I don't—Of course it got around the company you know, well, hah, 'the medic didn't do it'."
> "Did anyone report these incidents?"
> "No. No one did! You don't dare. Next time you're out in the field you won't come back—you'll come back in a body bag. What the hell, she's only a dink, a gook, this is what they think."[24]

Or consider this report of a Marine forward observer of one incident in a Vietnamese village:

> "The main thing was that if an operation was covered by the press there were certain things we weren't supposed to do, but if there was no press there, it was okay. I saw one case where a woman was shot by a sniper, one of our snipers. When we got up to her she was asking for water. And the lieutenant said to kill her. So he ripped off her clothes, they stabbed her in both breasts, then spread her eagle and shoved an 'E-tool' up her vagina, an entrenching tool, and she was still asking for water. And then they took that out and they used a tree limb and then she was shot."[25]

The hardened cynic might opt for the standard evasion that reports such as this are merely sensationalist pictures from far away; there were many at the time. But even those on the home front, outraged with and threatened by the facts of Vietnam, seemed inescapably sullied by the collective current of erotic violence. One of the most popular record albums known to the protester of the late sixties shouted out the lyrics:

> The killer awoke before dawn. He put his boots on.
> He took a face from the ancient gallery, and he walked on down the hall.
> He paid a visit to where his sister lived,
> And he paid a visit to his brother,
> And he walked on down the hall.
> And he came to a door, and he went inside . . .
> "Father?"
> "Yes son."
> "I want to kill you."
> "Mother, I want to . . . (screams) . . . come on babe . . . "[26]

With a shocking poetic justice both the horror as well as the specifically sexual violence of the Vietnam War were blended by Francis Ford Coppola with the strains of precisely this song by The Doors in his Vietnam-era flashback *Apocalypse Now*. The point being stressed in this is the inevitable collective involvement of one and all in the violence of an age. This is the spirit also of Susan Brownmiller's fundamental thesis, though the brunt falls on men:

> The Greek warrior Achilles used a swarm of men descended from ants, the Myrmidons, to do his bidding as hired henchmen in battle. Loyal and unquestioning, the Myrmidons served their master well, functioning in anonymity as effective agents of terror. Police-blotter rapists in a very real sense perform a Myrmidon function for all men in our society. Cloaked in myths that obscure their identity, they, too, function as anonymous agents of terror.[27]

Or again: "Rape . . . is nothing more or less than a conscious process of intimidation by which *all men* keep *all women* in a state of fear."[28]

Thus the full indictment, and with it not only grim scenes, a sense of fear and disgust, but—for the man with some sense of shadow who allows himself to be penetrated by the spirit of feminine rage—a compelling and sobering sense of involvement. So confronted, the masculine and feminine contents of one's psyche seem to choose sides, gazing at one another, uncomprehending. Of course the question may promptly and reasonably be raised from the masculine side as to whether an attack of this pitch is justified. This is like beginning with Original Sin! At this point, then, the debate can begin.

The following dream of a man in his mid-twenties clearly illustrates that the problem of rape is considerably more complicated in the unconscious than it appears in arguments of accusation and defense on the surface.

> It is years after the fact, but I stand accused of statutory rape for having had sexual relations with two girls. I go to court. Formal arrangements have been made and a serious hearing is at hand. I am very angry, but feel guilty and responsible. My father is the defending attorney.
>
> Upon arriving I am alone—away from my parents—and find myself in a room where I and the jury are "prepared" for the trial by two women deputies of the court who come around the room and do things to our eyes: first they shine a bright beam of ultraviolet light into each eye, and secondly they put one drop of purple liquid into our eyes. The jury is all women!
>
> Then a strange rough woman, rather young, whom I assume is another deputy of the court, takes me brusquely by the arm and leads me away—into custody, sort of. I figure we are on our way to the courtroom, *but* she begins to take me down into the most uncanny surroundings where there are criminals of all sorts and evil law enforcement officials brutalizing people. One policeman is shoving a dark man around and cursing him. The woman takes me to a place where I see many shops—blacksmith and chemistry shops from the Middle Ages. In the chemistry shop is a freakish turtle wiggling all about. Finally the woman takes me to a room where I am threatened with attack by a wild group of her intimate male companions.

Beneath the courtroom rationalism, which would seek to allot the blame for rape, are deep and convoluted questions. Certainly this dream may stand as a document of the reverberation of the question of rape in the contemporary psyche, but what equally concerns our present investigation is the strange "preparation" of eyes and the movement into symbolic depth. The dream reflects a need to seek a kind of "ultraviolet" vision—to adopt a perspective which would attempt to see through our problem to its basic chemistry. Indeed the turtle itself is an old alchemical image of the *prima materia,* the basic, original matter.

The contention that any man is a potential rapist is a sweeping statement which has sparked much controversy. Likewise is Susan Brownmiller's remark that *"all men* keep *all women"* in a state of fear and conscious intimidation. Lionel Tiger, a Rutgers University anthropology professor, some of whose terms were adopted by Brownmiller, responded in a *New York Times* review as follows: "The idea is splendid, the moral urgency is commendable, the practical discussion of policy alternative is necessary." He found the work, however, to be "deeply scarred by dreadful and simply wrong anthropology, not to mention highly questionable assumptions about human prehistory, psychology and usefulness of literary materials as metaphors for empirical life."[29] Mythology might well be added to this list. Though a minor point, Myrmidons were a race of men *and* women sprung from ants. Their king, though an ally of Achilles, had a daughter who herself was a victim of rape—by Zeus.[30] More significant is Brownmiller's general lack of awareness regarding mythology:

> People often ask what the classic Greek myths reveal about rape. Actually they reveal very little. For one thing myths about any given god or goddess are often contradictory and impossible to date; and for another, it is far too easy to retell a Greek myth to fit any interpretation one chooses. . . . It is more sensible, I think, to consider the Greek myths charming fables whose origins have been hopelessly lost and proceed to more tangible substances.[31]

While accepting the obvious need for the most cautious handling of myth, and considering Tiger's words regarding the usefulness of literary material as metaphors for empirical life, one must question Brownmiller's cursory dismissal of mythology, which for the depth psychologist provides a mass of data on the empirical life of the collective psyche. Brownmiller also makes a number of premature and uninformed assumptions, two of which are mentioned here. First is the notion that simply because she has attacked psychoanalysis for its more obvious sexist contents, she has thereby dealt with psychology. Second is her failure to differentiate Freudian Psychoanalysis, Adler's Individual Psychology, and Jung's Analytical Psychology, especially the considerable differences in their attitudes toward women. We shall return to psychoanalysis, to Jung and to mythology, but only after further reflections on the feminist position, the experience of the rape victim, and an examination of the most recent clinical findings on the psychology of men who rape.

Limitations of the Feminist Hardline

There are many reasons why, among some feminist writers such as Brownmiller, there is a vested interest in keeping all considerations of rape as unpsychological as possible. Prominent among these is the fact that insofar as feminism is a socio-political movement, it is founded upon a root fantasy of progress toward general social well-being through the gradual elimination of social ills—in the present case that of rape. In Brownmiller's approach this progressive ideal goes to the extreme in the most black and white manner, describing rape simply as a crime against women perpetrated fundamentally by all men. A popular self-defense handbook, *Against Rape,* by Medea and Thompson, warns also that any man is a potential rapist. Already examined is the way in which all men may to a degree share in a broadly defined collective guilt—a guilt perhaps of having male musculature, genitalia, or of simply living in a world where atrocities take place. It is true that rape is largely a crime against women, which can and must be curtailed through social action, but its victims include children, men as well as women and it is perpetrated by assailants of both sexes.

Two Massachusetts clinicians report that the results of their study "would suggest that the incidence of sexual offenses against children perpetrated by adult women is much greater than would be expected from the rare instances reported in the crime statistics."[32] In the same study it was found that nearly one-third of the rapists studied had themselves been subjected to some sexual trauma in their youth, by parents, siblings and relatives. The authors add that "since rapists were victimized more by females than by males, this may in part explain the victim selection of women as targets of their hostile sexual offenses."[33] Political manifestoes such as Brownmiller's depend on blanket statements and the closest approximation to an unequivocal set of judgments. But all political movements attempt to reinforce their position with the aid of projection. The sense of virtue, as well as the moral deficit ascribed to the opposition, is akin to the fantasy that the United States suddenly grew stronger and more unified in 1979 as its collective shadow came to rest on the heads of "barbarians" in Iran.

Obviously, more finely differentiated considerations of the problem of rape cannot maintain a radical indictment of men as a whole. The collective and concretistic view of rape by the socially and politically oriented is essential in its place. The psychological view, however, is necessarily preoccupied with the individual and with a relative conception of progress toward "well-being." Sexual violence and death are in themselves neutral facts of existence. As for the individual victim, the question is "Society who?," for statistical material is of psychological value only to the extent that it aids in an understanding of the individual soul. Should the person in question be a convicted rapist, his story might well be a compelling and tragic one. Although responsible for his actions before the law, he may well come from a broken home, have been the object of violence on the part of a drunken father, of sexual abuse by an incestuous mother, or have a history of cultural deprivation and alienation. This too, however, is looking at the individual in "micro-sociological" terms; rape may finally be an irreducible archetypal enactment intertwined with his unique fate and individuation.

Even in facing the rapist with the sobriety and firmness appropriate to the menace he is, one may well ask if the psychotherapist is here confronting merely—as Brownmiller would have it—one of "the front-line shock troops, terrorist guerillas in the longest sustained battle the world has ever known."[34] At such a moment of confrontation the militant feminist's systematic denial of all motivations in rape save that of power grows problematic and is shadowed by its own deficit of compassion. Violent though many rapes may be, "the sexual component of rape should not be downplayed in the haste today to accentuate the violent nature of the behavior."[35] However distorted or violent, rape is largely a question of sex, and of sex extending to love and the longing for acceptance and union.

Impressive indeed is the manner in which contemporary literature on rape, feminist as well as clinical, emphasizes again and again the male's reaction formation to repressed feminine qualities in himself; yet nowhere has a serious attempt been made to come to terms with the masculine element within women. Helene Deutsch, a favorite target of modern feminists for her allegiance to Freud, comes closest to describing the phenomenology of what C. G. Jung called the animus, the masculine side of a woman.[36] It is precisely the question of the animus which threatens with betrayal the integrity of the militant female crusader against men.

The case of feminist sociologist Diana E. H. Russell proves instructive of just this problem. Her book, *The Politics of Rape*, consists of a long series of interviews with rape victims and educates the reader in a strikingly first-hand manner on the nature of rape from the victim's perspective. It is a very useful work. Russell's commentary speaks of the rare desire among female rape victims to kill their assailants—and indeed women victims more generally feel a sense of guilt and responsibility than a reaction of immediate revenge—yet a considerable number of the very women interviewed express precisely their desire to kill rapists—a clear contradiction of her own views. In the course of her remarks, Russell also dissociates masochism from the feminine, while she retains sadism as characteristically masculine. Most impressive, late in the book after reflections on variations between men and women, is Russell's statement:

> If our culture considered it masculine to be gentle and sensitive, to be responsive to the needs of others, to abhor violence, domination and exploitation, to want sex only within a meaningful relationship, to be attracted by personality and character rather than by physical appearance, to value lasting rather than casual relationships, then rape would indeed be a deviant act, and I would think, much less frequent.[37]

She then proceeds to close her book with defense tactics and a final chapter entitled, "Solutions: Feminine Rage and Other Alternatives." The flaw in this representative attitude is obvious; on one hand the most unreal idealism and sentimentality is wistfully held forth and, on the other, a castrating revenge. The naiveté of even a university sociology professor is—in this case at least—quite remarkable.

Certainly rapists *are* mostly men, their victims primarily women— and no one should presume to detract from all the good which the feminist outcry against rape has accomplished in recent years. But, as stated above, the present psychological perspective concerns the psychology of rape and the *individual*—whether the angry feminist, the rapist or his victim—and particularly the meaning of rape as an intrapsychic event. Psychology, and especially the psychology of the unconscious, has always raised into the light of day factors which are initially disruptive to the hallowed certainties of consciousness and which often do give moral stances the most disquieting sense of suspension. Already in 1949 Simone de Beauvoir spoke critically of the fact that in psychoanalysis "morality is envisaged as foreign to sexuality,"[38] and lamented, "All psychoanalysts systematically reject the idea of choice and the correlated concept of value, and therein lies the intrinsic weakness of the system."[39] Choice, like the concept of liberty, was certainly a trespassed value in need of reassertion in the wake of World War II when de Beauvoir wrote *The Second Sex*. Yet Nazism proved more pointedly than any phenomenon of recent time the degree to which collective and basically impersonal factors wield a mighty power over men. Less intelligently in 1973, Susan Brownmiller renews de Beauvoir's complaint:

> But perhaps most critically, the serious failure of the Freudians stemmed from their rigid unwillingness to make a moral judgement. The major psychoanalytic thrust was always to "understand" what they preferred to call "deviant sexual behavior" but never to condemn.[40]

Regardless of how liable psychoanalysis may be for certain rigid or insufficient theoretical positions, that it should be expected to condemn rather than proceed as an experimental science is not only misleading, but amounts to a signpost of warning. Shall the botanist condemn the Venus Flytrap for being carnivorous? Without question the intention of psychoanalysis is to ·understand, and aiding this process will be a caution against its becoming a moralizing political tool. One may share Russell's abhorrence of violence, domination and exploitation, champion choice, value and liberty where they are battered concepts needed by society for its revitalization, or condemn "deviant sexual behavior," but the psychic phenomenon of rape will remain vital and archetypal, in men, in women, in the collective psyche.

The dream with which this study opened reflects the shadowy fact that even the most ardently held good intentions are, tragically but inevitably, insufficient. The contention of Brownmiller that "the rape fantasy exists in women as a man-made iceberg," and that it "can be destroyed—by feminism,"[41] is the product of a moralizing, collective and concretistic perspective. Appropriate though it might be to sociology or politics, it is and must be alien to any true attempt at a psychological exploration of the phenomenology of rape.

2

The Victim of Rape

A Life-Threatening Situation

Compelled as we are to remain close to the actual experience of the individual, our next step toward a psychological perspective shall be an examination of the victim's response. She may be anyone from a few months of age to 81 years, at least this is the eldest victim encountered in the present research. The assailant may be anyone, known or unknown, someone simply forcing a seduction to a sadistic rape-murderer. The setting of the attack may be one's own apartment, a car, a remote spot. In any case, current literature stresses that the victims' main emotional reaction at the time of the rape is fear. "They report being scared that they would be killed. The rape is clearly experienced by them as a life-threatening event."[42]

Informed of this general reaction—though perhaps most particularly from a male perspective—one senses some exaggeration. Anger, contempt, disgust would seem to be more likely, but the equation rape=death is recurrent in history. The rape of the Roman princess Lucretia by Tarquin spelled death—through suicide no less. A mythological figure in a strongly patriarchal context, Lucretia seeks to save the family honor. The theme of "the marriage of death" recurs historically in the work of painters like Lucas Cranach, Hans Baldung Grien, and Eduard Munch, as well as in the myths of Amor and Psyche, Demeter and Persephone, and reflects a deeper psychological background to this reaction. For the present, however, one is well advised to bear in mind the stark reality of the standard use of brute force, knives and hand-guns, and the commonplace verbal threats of death to which rapists resort.

Not surprisingly, rape victims seldom experience the assault as erotic. One Tennessee study of the erotic response to sexual assault with a sample of 50 women found that none had experienced orgasm.[43] The factor of the women's generally more gradual arousal in intercourse cannot sufficiently account for this; the traumatic nature of the situation is of far greater significance. For the male victim, confusion regarding his own sexual image may arise from a failure to distinguish between the physiological process of their forced ejaculation—commonly induced by men raping men—and the broader emotional experience of orgasm.[44] To what degree the assailant experiences the event as erotic varies dramatically, as will be seen in chapter four.

The Aftermath: Stigma and Stereotype

One great burden the female victim must carry as a component of her pain is the weight of collective prejudices and stereotyped conceptions about women who get raped. The stock phrases seem to be endless: "She asked for it!" "As long as you're being raped you might as well lie back and enjoy it!" "No woman can get raped against her will." "Women who get raped secretly long to be raped." Such remarks are the most obvious evidence that the responsibility for rape is projected onto women, and not only by the uneducated.[45] Truly, it is remarkable how quickly the strong will and vaunted integrity of men can simply evaporate before the question of responsibility in rape. The rape victim suffers from just this evasion. Considering the victim who is not only raped, but beaten, held with a weapon or threatened with death, the claim that "she asked for it" is manifestly absurd. This clear projection has a deep psychological background which will be a major focus of this study. The second and third of the above statements are likewise glib and unrealistic—part of the standard fair of insensitive chauvinist remarks. The idea that women secretly wish to be raped is a controversy in itself, as will be seen.

A rape victim, if she reports the assault, will encounter a number of difficult situations before she ever reaches a therapist's consultation room—for instance, visiting the police station. Burgess and Holmstrom describe their conversations with police officers in Boston:

> Police talk of rape as being a "terrible thing." One officer who sees rape as a very traumatic experience said he treats it "as if the victims were in a state of shock." An older officer said, "I have come to the conclusion that rape is the most heinous of crimes." They talk of rapists as being "perverted" or "animals." They say, "Something is wrong with these guys."[46]

> Officers tend to have a punitive attitude toward the rapist. Talking about what should happen to the rapist, officers often express a fantasy of what they would *like* to do to him: namely make a direct physical attack. One said: "You know, I have a daughter, in fact I have four daughters. If one of them had this experience . . . I would go after the man myself maybe. And you know what I would do? I would castrate the beast."[47]

Some of the men with whom the rape victim immediately comes in contact after the event will respond in this way; others are paternal, overly solicitous, or even cold. Typically, reactions vary greatly depending on the assumed sexual reputation of the woman in question. Law enforcement officials are, however, a bureaucracy—impersonal and primarily interested in having a case which will bring a conviction. The following profile of the "perfect victim" not only gives an idea of police criteria for a good case, but also serves as an example of one set of collective judgments by which the victim's integrity and credibility may be gauged.

> Putting their criteria together into an "ideal type" composite, the perfect case would be one in which all the information checks out, there are police witnesses to the crime, the victim can provide a good description of the assailant, there is supporting medical evidence including sperm and injuries, the story remains completely consistent and unchanging, the victim is forced to accompany the assailant, was previously minding her own business, a virgin, sober, stable emotionally, upset by the rape, did not know the offender and the assailant has a prison record and a long list of current charges against him.[48]

Difficulties for the victimized woman with a psychiatric history, a promiscuous sexual life, out on the town alone or hitchhiking by herself are quite evident. And the mentally ill and the retarded are common victims of sexual abuse.

Part of "joining the stereotype" includes encountering not only police reactions, but those of the victim's friends and relatives, whose responses range from understanding support to shocking insensitivity. In the same study just quoted Burgess and Holmstrom report:

> In approximately one fourth of the cases, people in the victim's network were more emotionally involved in pursuing the case than was the victim herself. This pattern was even more pronounced—occurring more than half the time—with preadult victims. For adult victims, it was almost always the males—boyfriends, husbands, fathers—who were more emotionally involved in pursuing the case than was the victim.[49]

The feelings of men near the victim may certainly include genuine sympathy, but the very notion of rape constellates many psychological factors: defenses spring up, incestuous claims are activated, conflicts arise between ego attitudes and the shadow's fascination with the crime; there are fantasies of violent retribution which display the typical proprietary attitude of men toward women and a sense of rivalry with the assailant. A woman's personal reactions may be largely neglected by those blinded by popular theoretical assumptions or preoccupied with their own needs. A case in point is that of a married 38-year-old mother of four from the midwestern United States. Ms. White was picked up after her car ran out of gas, was raped, beaten, and sustained lacerations; her claims were supported by laboratory tests. Her psychiatrist's first question?— "Haven't you really been rushing toward this very thing all your

life? You know, things don't just *happen,* you *make* them happen."[50]
Turning from insult to more injury, Ms. White was met with her
husband's response: "If that's what you wanted, why didn't you
come to *me!*"—before he raped her himself.[51]

Another phase of a woman's post-rape experience will likely consist of a medical examination, if not sought privately then as a
routine step in gathering legal evidence for the police. The victim
may be forced to spend considerable time in an emergency unit
accompanied by police, hospital personnel and acquaintances. Doc-
tors and nurses may also be caught up in stereotyped attitudes of
condemnation or solicitation. The major component of the medical
examination is a pelvic smear in order to verify the presence of
semen. (Actually the assumption that the presence of semen verifies
the rape is only partially sound, for in many rapes penetration
occurs without ejaculation.) This may be especially stressful, as Burgess and Holmstrom observe:

> The rape victim's body has just been violated sexually in a life assault.
> Thus invasive medical procedures may have special significance for
> her . . . the assault designed to injure and the medical procedure de-
> signed to help both invade the same site on the body.[52]

In one particular case, the physician, exasperated at his "uncoopera-
tive" patient, said, "If you tighten up, I'll really hurt you, I mean it.
Let go loose. . . . You've got to relax. It's very important." These
directions were similar to those of the rapist. The woman reported
that during the rape the assailant said, "If you're calm, I won't hurt
you."[53]

Should the victim of rape choose to press charges—a decision that
calls for considerable reflection—a confrontation with another bureaucracy awaits her. "The court experience for the rape victim,"
write Burgess and Holmstrom, "precipitates as much of a psychological crisis as the rape itself. Victims undergo a multitude of intense
reactions to specific features of court."[54]

Going to court in the course of a trial involves the frequent
repetition of details of the original incident, keeping the experience
alive when presumably a woman's wish would be to let it take its
place in the past. There may be threats, pressure to drop charges,
appeals, time delays (in the United States easily two years may
elapse from assault to verdict), as well as harassment from defense
attorneys. However predicated on the service of justice the courts
and the practice of law may be, the treatment of rape victims has no
shining tradition. Lawyers as much as any others may be imbued
with sexist notions against women in general and rape victims in
particular. The famous counselor Blackstone, whose caution on the

credibility of the female witness is still repeated in law schools, declares:

> If she be of evil fame and stand unsupported by others, if she conceal the injury for any considerable time after she had the opportunity to complain, if the place where the act was alleged to be committed was where it was possible she might have been heard and she made no outcry, these and the like circumstances carry a strong but not conclusive presumption that her testimony is false or feigned.[55]

Naturally a woman's testimony might be false, but behind these remarks are a number of prejudices a woman may face in pursuing her case. The defamation of plaintiffs is devastatingly effective, as the extremely low conviction rate for rape clearly shows. The stress and humiliation of the court process is such that, whatever the legal outcome, it constitutes one of the more important emotional experiences the rape victim brings to psychotherapy.

Given the various reactions to her situation, the rape victim may seek a therapist simply out of an urgent need to have her own personal reactions heard objectively—possibly for the first time. She (or he, we must remind ourselves) needs a refuge away from the collective, away from the personal network of friends and relatives who are subjectively involved. The responsible therapist has to be conscious of the problems already stated in the victim's previous contacts, sensitive to the physical concerns and typical psychological reactions, and—as is crucial—aware of the part played by his or her (the therapist's) own psychology in the analytical work.

A raped woman may sustain no physical injuries or, at the other extreme, be brutally and sadistically assaulted. This obviously affects the degree to which the rape was experienced as a life threat. Were it not for the fact that a great many women are protected by contraceptives, the major physical concern following rape would no doubt be the question of pregnancy.[56] Today, the concern over the possible contraction of venereal disease is no less prevalent. Although penicillin is routinely administered to the victim of sexual assault as a countermeasure, the fantasy of the possibility of venereal disease, like that of pregnancy, compounds the psychological impact of the rape experience, both in the most organic sense of being invaded by sinister forces and because these fears extend the psychological event in time. In light of this it is little wonder that a negative VD test and the recurrence of menstruation are crucial steps in recovery.

Typical Emotional Reactions

In recent years the typical emotional reactions of the rape victim have been much studied. An article by Sutherland and Scherl describes the initial reactions as shock, humiliation, fear, sadness and anxiety.

Though she may be moved with sufficient determination to desire full legal retribution, a second phase in adjustment is typically a self-protective retreat and introversion. According to the cited study, "Her interest in seeking help and talking about the experience wanes rapidly. This response is healthy and should be encouraged despite the fact that it represents an interim period of pseudoadjustment."[57] Someone has pointed out the similarity between the word "therapist" and "the rapist"—calling to mind what has been said of invasive medical procedures; hence the psychotherapist, regardless of sex, would do well to respect this retreating phase by foregoing an inclination to "penetrate defenses." The interiorization of the rape experience is both a natural self-protecting mechanism and an approach by which the ultimate significance of the rape for the person's life may be reached and experienced.

In like manner, the common and important guilt reaction—however greatly it may appear to be a product of collective prejudices regarding female responsibility for rape—is at this point an emotionally real part of the victim's response. Premature attempts to dispel these guilt feelings may, besides being useless, contaminate the therapeutic vessel with "feminist anger" or an equally destructive, proprietary goodwill of the therapist deficient in his sense of shadow. Overly "enlightened" approaches leave shadows; the rape victim needs neither to be joined in rage nor coddled by saviors.

A third phase of the emotional recovery is often marked by depression, renewed reflectiveness and the surfacing of anger.

> Her initial feelings of anger—denied, suppressed or rationalized during Phase 2—now reappear for resolution. Frequently her anger toward the assailant is distorted into anger toward herself which exacerbates the characteristic depression of this phase. Thus, it is important for the workers to permit the patient to express this anger.[58]

The resurgent anger is extremely important as a sign of renewed self-determination. Constructively dealt with by the patient, it serves not only as a movement out of the depression, but may be the fiery *prima materia* of a wider psychological development *through* the rape experience. Any event vividly occurring as a life-threatening experience carries the potential of being a life-changing and transformative experience in the deepest sense. To this we will turn a bit later.

An additional reaction to rape is flight, multi-determined by the fear of a second assault (which despite the common threats is rare), by guilt reaction, a need to find understanding elsewhere, general panic, etc. Burgess and Holmstrom remark that in their subjects the move in order to ensure safety and to facilitate the victims' ability to function in a normal style was very common. Forty-four of ninety-four victims changed residences within a relatively short time after the rape. There was also a strong need to get away, and some women took trips to other states or countries.[59]

It is striking the degree to which the experience of rape disrupts the external as well as the emotional life of the victim. Disrupted also may be eating patterns, attention to daytime responsibilities owing to recurrent fantasies which relive the rape from various angles, and also sleeping patterns. The Burgess and Holmstrom study found that "women who had been suddenly awakened from sleep by the assailant frequently found that they would wake each night at the time the attack had occurred. The victim might cry or scream out in her sleep."[60]

Victims' Dreams

This brings us to the question of dreams, to which the least amount of attention has been given in current literature on either rape victims or rapists themselves. Raped women frequently suffer nightmares and night-time anxiety, as in the following account.

> I had a terrifying nightmare and shook for two days. I was at work and there was this maniac killer in the store. He killed two of the salesgirls by slitting their throats. I'd gone to set the time clock and when I came back, the two girls were dead. I thought I was next. I had to go home. On the way I ran into the maniac killer and he was the man who attacked me—he looked like the man. One of the girls held back and said, "No, I'm staying here." I said I knew him and was going to fight him. At this point I awoke with a terrible fear of impending doom and fright. I knew the knife part was real because it was the same knife the man held to my throat.[61]

Thus the reverberation of the traumatic event within the psyche of one particular victim. Important to note is that though certain details —such as the appearance of "the maniac killer" resembling the assailant, and the knife—reflect the original event, the dream includes two salesgirls, a work situation, and the ambivalence between fear and attack as imaged by the dream-ego and one of the two girls.

Immediately discernible is the way in which the unconscious begins to weave material from the traumatic event with other images from the dreamer's daily life, spontaneously broadening and compounding the significance of the event. A careful regard for this spontaneous activity of the psyche is the core of the analytical work. Burgess and Holmstrom describe the dreams' elaborations, in however a rudimentary fashion, by pointing out two types of dreams they observed:

> One is similar to the above example where the victim wishes to do something but then wakes before acting. As time progressed, the second type occurred: the dream material changed somewhat, and frequently the victim reported mastery in the dream—being able to fight off the assailant. A young woman reported the following dream one month after her rape: "I had a knife and I was with the guy and I went to stab him and the knife bent. I did it again and he started bleeding and died. Then I walked away laughing with the knife in my hand."[62]

The dreamer woke up crying and frightened. Scanty though this material may be, the aforementioned resurgence of anger and self-assertion is plainly to be seen—an important sign. The dreamer's distress upon awakening from emotions of such powerful revenge display a strong aggressive impulse yet to be integrated. The dream may also help dispel the notion that such desires are absent in women.

The recovery from rape as it has been traced here reflects research of women whose own coping mechanisms were supported by relatively short treatments or follow-ups. One of my own former patients, however, a 65-year-old woman diagnosed schizophrenic, had suffered her first psychotic episode after being raped some 20 years before. This single example illustrates one of the more serious psychological difficulties that may result from sexual assault.

External Personifications of the Animus

Evident throughout is the tendency for the significance of rape to be compounded in the aftermath of the experience both by external factors and through the spontaneous imaginative activity of the psyche in recurrent dreams and fantasies. In like manner to the rings around a stone thrown in water, the rape experience touches complexes, taking on an ever more generalized (or all-embracing) meaning for the victim. Rape may, for example, expand into a grand metaphor of victim and oppressor. The surfacing anger, a tremendously important, potential agent of transformation, may easily be squandered in over-indulgent projection. The way in which this current of libido is channeled and psychologically worked on by patient and therapist is crucial. Therein, beyond recovery in the general sense, lies the possibility for a renewed perspective of the world.

Reviewing for a moment, one sees that following the initial encounter with the rapist, the victim has faced lover, husband, brother, father, police, doctor, lawyer, defense attorney and assailant again in court, the judge and any number of other men. In each of these contacts she is the center of attention owing to an invasion of the most private parts of her body and, more importantly, an invasion of her own psychological space. She has thus experienced the most varied external personifications of the animus, the archetypal masculine, in a uniquely personal way. An observation by Burgess and Holmstrom provides a fine pictorial sense of this:

> The judge may be seated on the bench or may sit at the head of a long and imposing table . . . flanked by flags, symbols of the power and authority of the state.
>   The costumes increase the ceremonial atmosphere of the occasion. The judge wears the traditional black robe, which Kessler suggests has a mystical significance. "The robe is a symbol of the role to be played by all persons in the situation . . . it is a convenient shorthand symbol for the institution of justice as a whole." At superior court, officers are dressed in blue and gold trimmed uniforms. Others—persons escorting the defendants in custody, some policemen, some witnesses—also may be in special uniform.[63]

In light of such pomp one can imagine how cutting it may be to face in court the pressures and possible humiliations already described. Alternatively, the entire experience may offer a unique, if difficult, opportunity for a correspondingly diverse reflection upon men and the many guises of that inescapable contrasexual figure, the animus. To this we shall return in chapter five.

3

A Review of Theories

Krafft-Ebing: Sexist and Concretistic

The intention of this chapter is not to provide a thorough history or extended critical comparison of psychological views, but to examine some theoretical contexts in which the rape problem has appeared and the manner in which it has been treated.

Psychology carries within it a legacy of misogyny which runs very deeply in the history of the collective psyche.[64] The will to power of the masculine spirit and the accompanying archetypal fear of women will later be examined. For historical evidence one need not look far—indeed, Krafft-Ebing has already been introduced. Though the tendency to look down on the shortcomings of men of earlier times easily leads to self-deception, the blindness displayed in the work of such a "scientific" authority is nevertheless remarkable.

Since Krafft-Ebing is the earliest author whose ideas on rape are here being presented, it is worth scrutinizing one especially transparent passage from his *Psychopathia Sexualis:*

> Where the husband forces the wife by menaces and other violent means to the conjugal act, we can no longer describe such as a normal physiological manifestation, but must ascribe it to sadistic impulses. It seems probable that this sadistic force is developed by the natural shyness and modesty of woman toward the aggressive manners of the male, especially during periods of married life and particularly where the husband is hypersexual. Woman no doubt derives pleasure from her innate coyness and the final victory of man affords her intense and refined gratification. Hence the recurrence of these little love comedies.[65]

Here the classic shift is made by the author, and apparently quite unconsciously. Male menacing and violence mysteriously "develop" outside the man in the "natural shyness and modesty" of women. The projection of responsibility rests on the woman in the traditional fashion—"she gave me of the tree, and I did eat."

The view of this husband-wife interaction falls pitiably short of being psychological because of its disregard of the phenomenon of projection. No explanation of the coy lady's provocative powers is attempted; indeed the question of power is altogether left out. Rather we have the root fantasies of "normal physiological manifestations" and the "hypersexual" man. Krafft-Ebing, like Freud, was

31

Viennese. His view of the "innate coyness" of women might reflect his social milieu, as his view of sexuality is likewise a child of his time. What seemed certain to Krafft-Ebing and most of his generation was that psychic life was founded on the body alone. The obvious concomitant of this was that psychic life was imagined in crude and concretistic terms.

The consequences of this for a discussion of rape are most important. For example, Krafft-Ebing's discussion of masochism includes the following views:

> In woman voluntary subjection to the opposite sex is a physiological phenomenon. Owing to her passive role in procreation and long existent social conditions, ideas of subjection are, in women, normally connected with the idea of sexual relations. They form, so to speak, the harmonics which determine the tone quality of feminine feeling. ...In connection with the passive role with which woman has been endowed by Nature, [this] has given her an instinctive inclination to voluntary subordination to man.[66]

Hence we are assured, even rather poetically, that women are passive procreators whose instinctive inclination to voluntary subordination is not only culturally conditioned but a physiological fact, a law of Nature. The doctor might have done well to imagine carrying a child for nine months or to reflect on the complete superfluity of the man in the ambiance of a woman's labor!

Krafft-Ebing's attitudes are more than the result of reducing psychological characteristics to physiology, or an extrapolation of the fact that the vagina is a receptive organ. His remarks illustrate the way in which an overly reductive and rationalistic theoretical position is accompanied by the progressive devaluation of women and the feminine. On a level less intellectual—if of course the above passage can be called such—the assertion of male power in rape is played out against the same psychological background with more obvious but by no means less sinister results. Krafft-Ebing cannot by any means be considered a rapist. But when explanatory psychological principles are reduced to somatic or anatomical processes, and where these principles remain split in terms such as body/psyche, impulse/object, inside/outside, then the possibility of perceiving the integral unity of psychological phenomena is precluded; and where a sexist concretism and literalism prevail there is a further proliferation of sexist mythology cloaked in scientific garb.

The battling opposition of sadism and masochism forms a central example of the rift inherited and passed on by writers such as Krafft-Ebing down to the present day. In many ways it is tragic that this should be the case, not least among them the fact that in Krafft-Ebing himself the initial unifying intuition appears. Summarily he remarks that sadism and masochism are "two different sides of the same psychical process" and "represent perfect counterparts."[67] His statements, however, refer ever and again to this polarity concretely played out between two people and appearing in a context of sexual perversion. Where he does discuss this dynamism within the psyche of an individual, the attempt is contaminated with concretistic identifications of activity, sadism and masculinity with the empirical man, and passivity, masochism and femininity with the woman. Set in these terms, the possibility of a deeper penetration is lost in his terminological carousel.

The rigid identification of woman with the qualitative terms "passive," "masochistic," "submissive," etc., has been frequently and rightly criticized, and needs no reinforcement here. We might better refer to some other happy intuitions of Krafft-Ebing, foregoing his concretism. He does cite examples where there is no acting out of sexual violence, due to a higher regard for the fantasy itself. One patient observes, "The thought of a comedy with paid prostitutes always seemed so silly and purposeless, for a person hired could never take the place of my imagination."[68] Fortunately this is a typical state of affairs! And in the context of a discussion of masochism it is stated that this phenomenon originates "from purely psychical elements"[69] and that in "ideal" masochism "the psychical perversion remains entirely within the sphere of imagination and fancy. . . ."[70] Remarks such as these are far from Krafft-Ebing's fundamental thesis that a female tendency toward voluntary subjection is a "physiological phenomenon." They form part of a more psychological current that flows into psychoanalysis and Jung's Analytical Psychology.

Psychology and Sexuality

Further psychological reflections on sexuality may serve at this point as groundwork for an examination of the few treatments of rape in Freudian-psychoanalytic literature. It must first be emphasized that from a psychological perspective the body is a psychological experience. This, however, is not to react to the reduction of sexuality to physiology by embracing the spiritualist's fantasy of the body as a mere projection or concretization of spirit. The growing popularity of theosophy and Eastern mysticism side by side with the exaggerated claims of material science at the turn of the century showed just this enantiodromian tendency at work. The individual soul is negated in either the physical or the spiritual extreme, and precisely this *anima media natura*—the individual soul—is the present concern.

In this personal intermediary sphere, where the physical and spiritual archetypes interweave, the individuation process proceeds.

As already mentioned with regard to male rape victims, there is a difference between the physiological process of ejaculation and the experience of orgasm, just as the secretion of lubricating fluids contrasts with the far broader physical and imaginative female experience of orgasm. Many persons are incapable of orgasm without the simultaneous play of emotionally-charged fantasy. As may be quite simply observed, the psyche's fantasies and dreams draw in the strands of creativity, love, power and violence, death as well as reproduction, both instinct and spirit—sexuality is indeed one with the entire range of psychic activity and contents. An observation of the significance of sexuality beyond physical reproduction appears in *Marriage: Dead or Alive,* by Adolf Guggenbühl-Craig:

> Very little of the time and energy that people give to sexuality has anything to do with begetting children. Sexual life begins in earliest childhood and ends only at the grave. By sexual life I understand sexual fantasies, masturbation and sexual play, as well as the actual sex act. Only a very small portion of sexual life is expressed in deeds. The greatest part consists of fantasies and dreams. That these have little to do with reproduction is obvious. What we seldom realize, however, is that even the most sexual deeds have little if anything to do with reproduction.[71]

Rape most certainly has no sense for physical reproduction. What meaning it has for the individuation process we shall later examine, but here the following dream of a 28-year-old Danish man forms an appropriate vignette to these first words on the broad psychological significance of sexuality. The dream occurred right after he had seen *From the Life of the Marionette,* a film by Ingmar Bergman which deals with the murder of a prostitute and a man's psychological background.

> I am with a companion stealing into a man's house. This is like some homosexual place—a "leather" [sadomasochistic] atmosphere. This man knows all about pornography—its history, its best authors, etc. A great pornographic author has been dead for eight years.
>
> I am walking then in an unearthly paradise garden on hedge-lined paths, lovely trees overhead. The setting was also like a room in a large science museum I once visited in which one can see fetuses in bottles, a plastic pregnant woman, and walk through a huge model cell and a heart that beats thanks to a tape recorder. There is another couple there on the tree-lined, flowery path of the garden, but I am completely captivated by a mysterious bluish-skinned woman. I feel the most all-pervading feeling toward her—lust, mad desire. We smoke and sniff euphoric powdered drugs as we stroll along. Then there is an orgy.

In a house in a darkened room a rock band is roaring as lights blink on and off casting spiderweb designs on the ceiling. . . . then, in a very mysterious room with a broad, heavy wooden canopy reminding me of something M. C. Escher might draw: heavy, complicated. The bed is spread with a rich, light blue comforter. I lie in it, rolling one way to deeply and luxuriously kiss one beautiful woman, then the other way to kiss yet another woman of many in the bed. What is very strange is that at one moment I have a hold of my genitals and see that they are made of bronze and look like an Indian trident or one of those Buddhist thunderbolts. I pull at it again and again.

The atmosphere grows very strange, uncanny. I think I hear the cry of a baby and the song of a small white bird. Jumping up I search around the room. There is a niche in the wall just to the left of a heavy wooden staircase. I open the door to the niche and there is an archway receding into the darkness—I think I hear the baby and the bird chirp from in there.

In this single dream experience we see the luxuriant diversity (or polymorphous nature) of sexuality: homosexuality, sadomasochism, pornography, ardent heterosexual impulses, imagery of a paradise garden, implicit questions of childbirth, associations to Eastern cult objects, etc. The ontological question "Wherefrom?" is posed to the spellbound dreamer by the symbolically meaningful images of niche, receding archway, the child and the chirping of an unseen bird. Such a dream is a spontaneous product of a psyche concerned with questions which can never be satisfactorily answered from a merely physiological view of sexuality and reproduction, nor by the far more imaginative but nevertheless reductive, rationalistic and finally biologically-based theories of Freud—to which we shall now turn.

Freudian Contributions and Limitations

Knowledgeable criticism of orthodox or classical psychoanalysis needs to aim not at a haphazard dismantling of Freudian theory, but at an attempt to *see through it* to its archetypal background.

However rigid the doctrine maintained by Freud and his circle, and whatever misogynous elements the system may contain, no essential progress is made by criticism locked into a similar concretistic and literalistic perspective. Although the pointed critiques of feminists such as de Beauvoir, Friedan or Brownmiller unquestionably provide important clarifications, they remain superficial owing to the same limited point of view. Both sides must be seen against their respective archetypal backgrounds and with a mind to their respective blind spots. Guggenbühl-Craig has commented that only Jungians can really understand psychoanalytic literature because they can read it mythologically. A heady statement, certainly, but if true, it is no less so regarding feminist writings.

Freud urged Jung to join him in making his sexual doctrine an "unshakeable bulwark" against "mysticism."[72] As Betty Friedan notes in a footnote to her chapter "The Sexual Solipcism of Sigmund Freud," Freud's mysticism nevertheless crept in, taking—as repressed psychic contents invariably do—a negative and rudimentary form. The reference is to a pact made between Freud and his close friend Wilhelm Fliess (or between the animas of the two men) centering on a numerological fantasy connected to the female menstrual cycle.[73] Then again, Freud would certainly be distraught at the degree to which his entire system has come to be regarded as a modern mythology. On the side of the hardline feminist critique of psychoanalysis, the predictable reaction to a psychology based on the primacy of the penis may be seen: all men are rapists and oppressors, women are the innocent oppressed. At worst, animus and shadow remain repressed from consciousness and a blinding current of female rage takes the woman by storm.

In pursuing a truly psychological view of sexuality in general and of rape in particular, a major Freudian contribution must be borne in mind, as Guggenbühl-Craig points out:

> It is the merit of Freud's theory that sexual deviations are included in the understanding of sexuality and that the narrow understanding of sexuality is broadened beyond its connection to reproduction.[74]

One famous example of this is the so-called polymorphous-perverse child, Freud's model for the origin of all sexual behavior. The very fact that Freud never worked with children but based this theoretical notion on a reduction of the peculiarities of adult sexuality to the child is itself suspicious. Although the actual child provided the hook for Freud's fantasy of the origin of sexuality, the source of the conception has already been suggested by the dream of the young Dane quoted in the previous section. A florid array of sexual imagery flows to a lysis of the chirping white bird, receding darkness and the crying of an unseen child. The dream includes religious associations, a vision of paradise, numerous bottled fetuses decreasing in size, a cell, a heartbeat. These do not lead back to the empirical child, nor to the body and bloodstream of the personal mother to whom Freud commonly traced the regression of the libido, but to something beyond. Freud came to a similar threshold in his pursuit of the origin of sexual life. At the close of a late essay, "Beyond the Pleasure Principle," he grapples with the problems of Eros (love, or life instinct) and Thanatos (the death instinct) as far as his scientific reasoning could take him before capitulating:

Science has so little to tell us about the origin of sexuality that we can liken the problem to a darkness into which not so much as a ray of a hypothesis has penetrated. In quite a different region, it is true, we *do* meet with such a hypothesis; but it is of so fantastic a kind—a myth rather than a scientific explanation—that I should not venture to produce it here, were it not that it fulfills precisely the one condition whose fulfillment we desire. For it traces the origin of an instinct to *a need to restore an earlier state of things.*

What I have in mind is, of course, the theory which Plato puts into the mouth of Aristophanes in the *Symposium*, and which deals not only with the *origin* of the sexual instinct but also with the most important of its variations in relation to its object. "The original human nature was not like the present, but different. In the first place, the sexes were originally three in number, not two as they are now; there was man, woman, and the union of the two. . . . " Everything about these primeval men was double: they had four hands and four feet, two faces, two privy parts, and so on. Eventually Zeus decided to cut these men in two, "like a sorb-apple which is halved for pickling." After the division had been made, "the two parts of man, each desiring his other half, came together and threw their arms about one another eager to grow into one."[75]

Freud speaks here of the darkness which veils the origin of sexual life—the abyss of the unconscious psyche where no scientific theory can penetrate. The young man's dream as well as Plato's theoretical androgyne offer irreducible symbolic images of the unitary origin of life. Left with "a myth rather than a scientific explanation," the way clears toward a perception of the archetypal root of sexuality in all its diverse forms.

Retreating altogether from the expectation of finding a scientific answer to the origin of life or of sexuality, the question becomes one of what the psyche says of itself in its own language—and this with regard to sexuality and to rape. Freud speaks of "a need to restore an earlier state of things" and associated this with the death instinct. Discarding this notion of entropy and Freud's fundamental material-

Androgyne or hermaphrodite as union of opposites ("The sexes were originally three in number . . . man, woman, and the union of the two."—Plato's *Symposium*). —From *Hermaphroditisches Sonn- und Mondskind,* 1752.

ism, this primal condition may be taken *symbolically*. In the fantasy of the polymorphous-perverse child, as in the image of the Platonic androgyne, the "variations in relation to its object" characteristic of Eros coalesce into a single image of that dynamic monad, the Self, archetype of wholeness. The fact that the various relations between Eros and its objects can be reflected upon and experienced as numinous intrapsychic factors is the cornerstone of the present study. The instinctual tendency toward a primal condition may certainly appear as a regression in the pathological sense, but is ultimately nothing less than the gyroscopic intentionality of the individuation process which would bring the personality a deep sense of its primal wholeness.

Rape as a crime and a male problem has received the minimum of attention from psychoanalysis, nor did Jung ever deal with it specifically,[76] though he does provide a far richer model with which to explore the problem. Aside from the most basic limitation of Freud's system just discussed, he and other psychoanalytic writers continued to propound a theoretical view encumbered with overly personalistic notions of passive, feminine masochism and active, male sadism. Freud was most convinced that "feminine masochism . . . is the one that is most accessible to our observation and least problematic."[77] In his paper "The Economic Problem of Masochism," three forms of masochism—"erotogenic," "feminine" and "moral"—are again ultimately explainable in biological terms. Curiously enough, Freud's remarks about feminine masochism are restricted to a discussion of *men* in whom this is associated with "infantilism" which, owing to the accompanying guilt, leads to moral masochism:

> But if one has an opportunity of studying cases in which the masochistic fantasies have been especially richly elaborated, one quickly discovers that they place the subject in a characteristically female situation; they signify, that is, being castrated, or copulated with, or giving birth to a baby.[78]

As will be evident in the dream material to be examined, this theoretical formulation corresponds to a common and very real psychic phenomenon. The rigid maintenance of the personalistic identification of "feminine" with its pejorative tone, however, has not only provoked feminist writers, but also neglects archetypal factors such as the completely natural partial identity of a man with the anima, his feminine side. The dynamics of the libido which Freud describes in the old terminology in this essay correspond to the self-compensating play of introversion and extraversion—a phenomenon not bound by the qualitative "masculine" and "feminine," much less reducible to biology. Furthermore, a notion of morally masochistic, guilty infantilism constitutes the most rudimentary formulation possible of the ego's sense of inadequacy vis-à-vis the superordinate personality of the Self whose major manifestation is *conscience*.

In the writings of Helene Deutsch, the rape fantasies of adolescent girls are said to reflect the deep masochistic tendency of women:

> The fantasy life of girls in puberty reveals an unmistakable masochistic content. Girlish fantasies relating to rape often remain unconscious but evince their content in dreams, sometimes in symptoms, and often accompany masturbating actions. In dreams the rape is symbolic: the terrifying male persecutor with knife in hand, the burglar who breaks in at the window, the thief who steals the particularly valuable object, are the most frequently recurring figures in the dreams of young girls.
>
> The conscious masochistic rape fantasies, however, are connected with masturbation. They are less genital in character than the symbolic dreams, and involve blows and humiliations, in fact, in rare cases the genitals themselves are the target of the act of violence. In other cases they are less cruel, and the attack as well as the overpowering of the girls will constitute the erotic element.[79]

Once again talk of an "unmistakable masochistic content" appears; it evoked lively criticism in 1944, as it does today, for its sole correlation of these qualities with women. Deutsch attempts numerous clarifications:

> If we replace the expression "turn toward passivity" by "activity directed inward," the term "feminine passivity" acquires a more vital content, and the ideas of inactivity, emptiness, and immobility are eliminated from its connotations. The term "activity directed inward" indicates a function, expresses something positive, and can satisfy the feminists among us who often feel that the term "feminine passivity" has derogatory implications. . . . to reassure the reader we shall anticipate our discussion of feminine masochism by pointing out that it lacks the cruelty, destructive drive, suffering, and pain by which masochism manifests itself in perversions and neuroses.[80]

On the one hand Deutsch maintains the strongest allegiance to her psychoanalytic tradition in pursuing the subject of feminine masochism. But in her attempt to placate feminist critics she makes a crucial concession. Coining the neutral term "activity directed inward" she does shift away from the older sexist terminology, but she also empties her concept of masochism of cruelty, destructive drive and pain—thereby undercutting an already tenuous term. It must be recognized however that, conservative though she may have been, Deutsch was too psychological and too knowledgeable of the role of the masculine element in the female unconscious to fly to the opposite extreme, as exemplified by the attitudes of Diana E. H. Russell (referred to in chapter one).

One reads in Deutsch's discussion of young girls that "in dreams rape is symbolic"—a claim acceptable enough. Questionable, however, is just what is being symbolized. One need be cautious, for the latent content of dreams has a nasty habit of being bits of psychoanalytic doctrine. To simply interpret the male persecutor with the knife, the burglar at the window or the thief who steals a particularly valuable object as images of rapists (or, for that matter, the animus) is plainly inadequate, for each figure must be confronted regarding its unique plastic representation and affective component. Despite the fact that her examples image no sexual interaction at all, she can only refer to them as "genital" given her psychoanalytic formula. The unconscious rape fantasies she mentions are no more genital and her "conscious masochistic rape fantasies" are no less symbolic.

Deutsch reapproaches the problem of rape from various angles, one of which offers more material from which to consider the image of the raping male in women. In the following passage from *The Psychology of Women,* she includes a rape fantasy of her own:

> It is no exaggeration to say that among all living creatures only man, because of his prehensile appendages, is capable of rape in the full meaning of this term—that is, sexual possession of the female against her will. Every time I see one of the numerous pictures in popular movies or magazines showing an anthropomorphous ape or powerful, bearlike creature with a completely helpless female in his arms, I am reminded of my old favorite speculation: thus it was that primitive man took possession of woman and subjected her to his sexual desires. Interestingly enough in many myths and fantasy formations brutal possession is interpreted as a kindly act of rescue. Thus the ape with his powerful arms, or the bear, saves the girl from a threatening disaster that is mostly of a sexual nature—and the threat comes from somebody else, not from the rescuer. In young girls' dreams the mighty hairy human-animal figure often appears not as a seducer, but as a savior from sexual dangers. The metamorphosis of the seducer into savior reveals the wish-fulfilling character of the girl's dreams and her masochistic longings, which reproduce the situation of the primitive conquered woman.[81]

She goes on from this line of thought to speculations on how this eventually became a matter of pleasure to women. All in all this is a very concrete evolutionary fantasy. Deutsch, like her critic Brownmiller, follows sexual history back to the rough embraces of the powerful male.

Leda and the swan. — Museo Archaeologico, Palazzo Ducale, Venice.

Interestingly enough this parallels the Freudian fantasy of the ontology of individual sexual conflicts in the "primal scene"—parental intercourse considered a violent treatment of the mother by observing children. It is amazing how much peering into mommy and daddy's bedroom apparently went on in old Vienna. Whether or not this was sufficient to imprint a universal pattern in the human psyche remains doubtful. Deutsch points out how often myths and fantasy formations show brutal possession as an act of final rescue. This does not constitute a sellout to the erroneous and mundane notion that all women secretly long to be raped. Even a woman whose consciously elaborated sexual fantasy includes beating, binding, brutal rape or even dismemberment by no means actually *wants* to be raped. It is high time this was realized. Rather, Deutsch's description fits the ubiquitous polar phenomenology of the animus, as we shall see in chapter five.

Unfortunately Deutsch displays a concretistic and extremely superficial understanding of myth, speculating for example that the myth of Zeus as a swan, tickling and seducing Leda, sprang from some ancient scene in which "the powerful embrace of the prehensile arms, combined with the defensive counter-pressure produced strong pleasure sensations in the woman's entire body."[82] Of course, that which threatens, then makes its entrance, simultaneously does away with the threat and may spell pleasure or pain or a numinous third possibility. Facetious though it may sound in a discussion of rape, this characterizes any psychological relationship: that between the ego defending its own position and any autonomous psychic content such as a personal complex, the shadow, anima/animus or even the Self.

Recalling for a moment the question of inward-directed libido concomitant with the appearance of dream or fantasy images of the sinister male in various guises—as persecutor, burglar, thief, ape or other wild animal—one sees this including both an erotic aspect and a cruel destructive drive. Deutsch might well have alluded to the evil wizard in the Grimm fairytale "Fitcher's Bird," in whose forbidden room the first two of three sisters he lures away from home are cruelly murdered and cut in pieces before magically coming back to life, or again to any of the variations of "Beauty and the Beast." The story of Amor (or Eros) and Psyche as well portrays the fear of love and death, the transformative cruelty which may accompany a confrontation with the unconscious. This old tale, involving a marriage with death and the progressive differentiation of the masculine figure, has been the subject of works by both Erich Neumann[83] and Marie-Louise von Franz.[84] From the form of a fearful black snake, the masculine partner Eros rises to the Olympian pole of the spirit with Psyche joining him as his bride.

In concrete rape there is, of course, no question of a savior, but rather the brutal and assaultive appearance of the male on the blind instinctual level. A therapeutic perspective may consider such a concrete invasion as a parallel to Deutsch's examples, the evil wizard, the beast, or a deadly marriage which, beyond recovery in the general sense, yet carries the potential for psychological development.

The Archetypal Feminine in Rape

So far, only the role of the man and the masculine in rape has been considered. What role, if any, is played by the archetypal feminine in rape or dreams and fantasies of rape?

With regard to the inevitable feminist protest to such a notion nothing more need be said. An immense ambivalence naturally characterizes the young woman's approach to her defloration, her initiation into womanhood. A variety of the invading images of the male, which psychoanalysis would reduce to the penis, have already been seen, but it would be a presumptuous error to assume that this

Psyche throwing light on Amor (Eros).—Original drawing by Canadian artist Anne B. Knoop.

is the sole element in the initiation of a young woman. Simone de Beauvoir speaks of how "the idea of penetration acquires its obscene and humiliating sense within a more general frame, of which it is, in turn, an essential element."[85] In continuing to describe this broader background de Beauvoir paraphrases the following observation from Helene Deutsch:

> Another very frequent rape fantasy is a sort of masochistic orgy within a triangular situation. In this characteristic fantasy a female figure forces the girl to submit to sexual acts performed by men whom the female urges on. The female figure ties the girl, gags her, and prepares red-hot objects; these are applied by the men to the girl's genitals. Sometimes the female figure introduces a number of men who one after the other abuse the girl sexually. Compulsion by a woman plays a principal part in these practices. The superficial elements of these fantasies are easy to grasp: the pain decreases the guilt feelings produced by the pleasure, rape frees the girl from responsibility, the compulsion exerted by the woman, who represents the mother, is a counterweight to the latter's prohibitions.[86]

Here masculine figures are not the sole perpetrators of the rape, nor even the ones who initiate it. Deutsch proceeds to discuss the manner in which such fantasies spring from surfacing or repressed erotic needs. Indeed, as she says, the superficial elements of these fantasies are easy to grasp; they bespeak the ambivalence of budding sexuality, though their extreme nature suggests something of a neurotic relationship to it. She remains very personalistic in speaking of a counterweight to the mother's prohibitions, and her identification of the anonymous woman and the mother is only partially warranted, as will be seen.

Such phenomenology is by no means restricted to the psychology of women. The following dream of a man in his late twenties clearly corresponds, which is to say it arises from the same archetypal source:

> I see an attractive woman—a mother—and I see at the same time a lovely fluttering pink grosbeak. But something is wrong!
>
> Then I see the mother-woman and her young daughter, who is pink-cheeked and pretty. A bit of pink coloring is around the daughter as if it were coloring or little feathers from the bird. The mother gets enraged with the daughter and, casting her to the ground, tears her clothes. Then she tears the daughter's dress way open and leaves her trembling and naked. She then throws her in the path and wildly throws cooking oil all over her daughter's body as if to lubricate her. Three young boys are coming up the path and somewhat in a trance. They see this opportunity to experience sex for the first time—they begin to loosen their pants over the girl. They rape her.

In his article "The Psychological Aspects of the Kore," Jung describes the same phenomenon:

> The maiden's helplessness exposes her to all sorts of *dangers,* for instance of being devoured by reptiles or ritually slaughtered like a beast of sacrifice. Often there are bloody, cruel, even obscene *orgies* to which the innocent child falls victim. Sometimes it is a true *nekyia,* a descent into Hades and a quest for the "treasure hard to attain," occasionally connected with orgiastic rites or offerings of menstrual blood to the moon. Oddly enough, the various tortures and obscenities are carried out by an "Earth Mother." There are *drinkings of blood* and *bathings in blood,* also crucifixions.[87]

Violent forces presided over by a woman appeared also in the courtroom basement of the dream quoted earlier, in chapter one. The three additional examples given here indicate that the split between the suffering Kore maiden (whether an aspect of the Self in women or of the male anima) and the mother is a recurrent psychic phenomenon.

Helene Deutsch gives a sense of the quality of the split in woman, as well as intuiting something beyond it. Referring to "the desire to be raped" and the emotions of surfacing sexual drive, she discusses the qualities of the daughter:

They are so fundamentally different from the emotional manifestations of motherhood that we are compelled to accept the opposition of
sexuality and eroticism on one hand, and reproductive instinct and
motherhood on the other. Thus the double sexual role of woman
expresses itself in the beginning, when we can see the psychologic
manifestations of both at the same time . . . we shall see how sexuality
and motherhood are often in absolute emotional contradiction, and
how they nevertheless merge in the deeper unconscious life of the
soul.[88]

The significance for men of this opposition between the reproductive mother and the erotic maiden will be examined below. The
convergence of these ostensibly contradictory qualities in the deeper
life of a woman's soul has been explored in a penetrating psychological study, "The Demeter-Persephone Mythologem with Reference
to Neurosis and Treatment," by Patricia Berry.[89] Gaia is Earth, and
her role in the myth of Demeter and Persephone may be said to
conform to that of the presiding mother or "Earth Mother" in the
preceding material. As the maiden, whom one may imagine is
pink-cheeked and virginal, picks flowers she is abducted by Hades
and carried off into the underworld on a pathway *opened by Gaia
herself.* Deutsch as well as Karen Horney speaks of "the homosexual
period of girls' early puberty";[90] their innocent narcissism is reflected in the myth by their gathering of narcissus flowers. Yet the
pursuit of the flower is simultaneous with "a strong heterosexual
attack."[91] Deutsch is speaking concretely, while the myth shows
Hades or Dionysos within the psyche; Horney analyzes the case of a
woman "who till late in life felt herself one with her mother" and in
whose psyche rape fantasies flourished.[92] Here the daughter had
never gone the initiatory way of the Kore.

Though Demeter and Kore correspond rather well to their human
counterparts, mother and daughter, it must be borne in mind that all
human beings, regardless of sex, are dwarfed by the gods and goddesses. For this very reason concretistic and personalistic conceptions
of the archetypal factors governing the life of the soul are inadequate. Worse, such false designations imply a psychological world
merely human in its scope. Evident throughout the preceding discussion is the unending conflict between men and women which this
myopia supports. An extremely important archetypal perspective is
achieved by Patricia Berry who, quoting Kerényi, explains:

We find the Gaia role expressed by Kerényi: " . . . the patient, earthly
endurance of the absolute mother is wholly lacking to her (the
maiden). It is not without reason that Gaia aids and abets the seducer
in the Homeric Hymn. From the Earth Mother's point of view, neither seduction nor death is the least bit tragic or even dramatic."
From the Gaia perspective the rape is not only "undramatic"; it is

evidently intentional. So we might conclude that somehow the rape fulfills Gaia's own nature in its underworld aspect. From the very beginning of the tale, as the Homeric text tells us, the maiden's rape is accomplished in accordance with the intentionality, or telos, of Gaia— Persephone's own great-grandmother, and the matrix of the entire feminine constellation.[93]

Helene Deutsch pondered how the sexuality and eroticism of the younger woman conflict with the reproductive instincts of the mother, yet "merge in the deeper unconscious life of the soul." Berry proceeds down the dark hall to an essential perception of the completely impersonal background of the mystery of feminine sexuality and the fantasy of rape.

To images and reflections of the polarity between reproductive mother and erotic daughter, and the significance of the Great Goddess in masculine psychology, the present study will return. The point has now been reached at which the insights gained may be carried into a consideration of the psychology of the rapist specifically. A review of clinical observations will provide the necessary ground on which to proceed.

The rape of Persephone by Hades.—Greek bas-relief.

4

The Psychology of the Rapist

Clinical Studies Compared

It happened that in Vienna a garish magazine cover caught my eye:
"Cock Rapers! Sex Crazed Women Prowling the Night Hungry for
Men!" Women, as is well known, have always borne the responsibility for rape, but this headline goes to a new extreme. This is a result
of the near-universal evasion of the problem by men, but springs
more essentially from man's experience of the feminine as an inner
factor.

The extent to which stereotypical popular attitudes join hands
with the most highly vaunted scientific pronouncements to condemn
the woman is truly remarkable. A clear example of this, and the
identification of man's experience of the feminine solely with actual
women, is a 1954 Rorschach study of rapists by the psychoanalyst
and criminologist Dr. David Abrahamsen, reported by Brownmiller:

> The conclusions reached were that the wives of the sex offenders on
> the surface behaved toward men in a submissive and masochistic way
> but latently denied their femininity and showed an aggressive mascu-
> line orientation; they unconsciously invited sexual aggression, only to
> respond to it with coolness and rejection. They stimulated their hus-
> bands into attempts to prove themselves, attempts which necessarily
> ended in frustration and increased their husbands' own doubts about
> their masculinity. In doing so, the wives unknowingly continued the
> type of relationship the offender had had with his mother. There can
> be no doubt that the sexual frustration *which the wives caused* is one
> of the factors in motivating rape, which might be tentatively described
> as a displaced attempt to force a seductive but rejecting mother into
> submission.[94]

The dynamics are recognizable and the problematic polarity between mother and sexual partner is plainly observed, but owing to
the narrow and concretistic theoretical perspective—to say nothing of
the author's enormous male presumption—the effect is no different
than that of Krafft-Ebing's, where the sadistic violence of the husband is mysteriously *caused* by the wife.

All clinical studies on rapists, regardless of sample and criteria of
assessment, describe men who are weak, inadequate, unsure of their
masculinity and usually socially maladapted. Criteria of assessment
however do vary markedly. The authors of one Massachusetts study
of institutionalized "sexually dangerous persons" display considera-

47

ble lack of clarity in just this regard. Among those *not* considered are "the disappointed young lover misunderstanding the glances of a young girl as a seductive invitation and arrested for accosting," and "the man on a date sexually provoked" into "a sudden, uncharacteristic, explosive rape." The reader must inevitably remain puzzled when the authors turn from these omissions to report that "the patient seen at the center shows serious defects in social relationships and social skills, lacunae in moral and ethical attitudes, impulse control functions that are tenuous and break down under relatively normal life stresses, [and] ego functions . . . that seem entirely intact until. . . . "[95] Indeed, a great number of offenders are left out of account in the preoccupation with the hard-core, court-committed "sexually dangerous persons."

The same authors observe "no congruence between rape and any specific diagnostic category," and declare that "all types of character neuroses, character disorders, and more severe borderline and psychotic states are represented."[96] Called to mind by these modern clinical observations is Krafft-Ebing's restricted view of the rapist as a "degenerate moral imbecile," a view these authors correct and refine. They criticize purely behavioral approaches and recognize that "the act of rape clearly cannot be understood unidimensionally simply in terms of motivation or in fact in terms of any single factor."[97] The two major factors they do consider—sexuality and power—appear intermingled in the psychology of the rapist, but not to such an extent as to disallow the general categorization of these into three general groups:

> Descriptively, the act of rape involves both an aggressive and a sexual component. In any particular sexual assault the part played by these impulses can be quite different. The primary aim may be hostile and destructive so that the sexual behavior is in the service of an aggressive impulse. In other instances the sexual motive is the dominating motive, and the aggressive aspect of the assault is primarily in the service of the sexual aim. In a third the two impulses are less differentiated, and the relationship between them can best be described as sexual sadism.[98]

The authors distinguish the three groups with their respective qualities of personality, emotional state and crime as follows:

I. Aggressive Aim

— emotional state of anger
— use of aggression to humiliate, dirty or defile victim
— involves biting, butting, tearing of genitals or breasts, rupture of anus through violent insertion of objects, etc.
— victims always complete strangers
— displacement of rage from mother or other woman onto victim
— often married or dating

- frequent pre- or postpubertal sexual trauma with older woman (often mother)
- some paranoid features

II. Sex Aim

- relative absence of violence, or any of the characteristic brutality of the first group
- not impulsive
- absence of paranoid features
- recurrent fantasies of performing well and receiving love
- more involved in perversions
- intensely repressed homosexuality
- socially compliant

III. Sex-Aggression Diffusion

- typical inability to experience sexual excitation without some degree of violence being involved
- no visible anger
- greatest degree of paranoid features
- physically and psychologically cruel parents

Many of the theoretical perspectives of this study are borrowed from the Freudian-oriented criminologist Manfred Guttmacher.[99] Its psychoanalytic bias is evident in both the conception of rape as an explosive expression of pent-up sexual impulses and the attention given to the overcompensation for repressed or latent homosexuality. The authors quote Guttmacher's version of the "Aggressive Aim" individual, who *"paradoxically* is not a sex offender" but rather "an aggressive, antisocial criminal who, like the soldier of a conquering army, is out to pillage and rob."[100] Like Guttmacher, the authors well recognize the intermingling of motivations in their "Sex-Aggression Diffusion" group, but throughout incline more to the sexual interpretation. This stands in the mainstream of the one-sided psychoanalytic tradition.

The choice of one of two—sexuality, or power and aggression—rather than a scientifically unacceptable paradox was made by Freud long before he wrote "Beyond the Pleasure Principle." Already in *Three Essays on the Theory of Sexuality* (1905) he struggled with the problem:

> The history of human civilization shows beyond any doubt that there is an intimate connection between cruelty and the sexual instinct; but nothing has been done toward explaining the connection, apart from laying emphasis on the aggressive factor in the libido. According to some authorities this aggressive element of the sexual instinct is in reality a relic of cannibalistic desires—that is, it is a contribution derived from the apparatus for obtaining mastery, which is concerned with the satisfaction of the other and, ontogenetically, the older of the great instinctual needs.[101]

Opting for what he holds to be "ontogenetically the older of the great instinctual needs" (i.e., Eros), Freud sees others more concerned with the aggressive component. One day this other instinct of "mastery"—the will to power—would find its prime exponent in Alfred Adler. As one may see, the same old debate appears in contemporary literature about rape.

A second clinical study of much greater breadth, clarity and detail, *Men Who Rape* by A. Nicholaus Groth and H. Jean Birnbaum, reports findings similar to those of the Massachusetts group. The authors' theoretical perspective, however, sharply contrasts in its emphasis on power in sexual assault. A heading, "Rape: A Pseudo-Sexual Act," precedes the following excerpt from this work:

> A number of popular notions and stereotyped images persist in regard to the offender, his victim, and the offense. With regard to the offender, he is frequently regarded as a lusty male who is the victim of a provocative and vindictive woman, or he is seen as a sexually frustrated man reacting under the pressure of his pent-up needs, or he is thought to be a demented sexfiend harboring insatiable and perverted desires. All these views share a common misconception: they all assume that the offender's behavior is *primarily* motivated by *sexual* desire and that rape is directed toward gratifying only this sexual need.
>
> Quite to the contrary, careful clinical study of offenders reveals that rape is in fact serving primarily nonsexual needs. It is the sexual expression of power and anger. Forcible sexual assault is motivated more by retaliatory and compensatory motives than by sexual ones. Rape is a pseudo-sexual act, complex and multi-determined, but addressing issues of hostility (anger) and control (power) more than passion (sexuality). To regard rape as an expression of sexual desire is not only an inaccurate notion but also an insidious assumption, for it results in the shifting of the responsibility for the offence in large part from the offender to the victim."[102]

Clearly this perspective differs from that of the preceding study. Groth and Birnbaum shift to the power perspective and their grouping of rapist types includes no "Sex Aim" designation. Rather, they classify rapes as "anger," "power" and "sadistic," though despite these titles the different authors' groupings do overlap. Groth and Birnbaum's "anger" type corresponds with the former study's "Aggressive Aim" group in that the assailants, in a state of intense anger, use considerably more force than needed to accomplish the sex act. They displace rage toward women, mother, wife, girlfriend, onto an anonymous victim and inflict considerable injury. Groth and Birnbaum point out also the relative lack of erotic fantasy of this type of assailant. Indicative of how meaningless the personal identity of the particular woman is for the "anger" rapist is his common inability to even recognize the victim in court. Groth and

Birnbaum's "sadistic" group corresponds generally with the former investigators' "Sex-Aggression Diffusion" designation.

The most interesting point of comparison between the two studies is that the characteristic features noted by the Massachusetts four under "Sex Aim" correspond, curiously enough, with those placed by Groth and Birnbaum under the heading of "power"! Common characteristics of the respective groupings include the use of force sufficient only to accomplish the sex act, florid and obsessive sexual fantasies both during the act and preceding it, fantasies of performing well and receiving love from the victim, preplanned rather than impulsive attacks, the presence of intensely repressed homosexuality or the conscious preoccupation with threatening homosexual ideas. Groth and Birnbaum note in their grouping that there is typically disappointment at the assault not living up to the elaborated fantasy and, as an extension of this, that a compulsive series of rapes may be set off in a search for the "right one." The assailant may also be sexually inquisitive, asking questions concerning the quality of his performance. Though many elements of this rapist type tally with the former study's "Sex Aim" group, Groth and Birnbaum stress the theme of dominance, capture, control and the assertion of masculinity. They point out that victims are sometimes kidnapped, held and raped repeatedly, and that the rapist may try to extend his control by gaining information about the victim or threatening future action.[103]

Recall the statement in the Massachusetts study that "paradoxically" some rapists are not sex criminals but more like soldiers in a conquering army. Groth and Birnbaum, from their own theoretical position of power, ponder exactly the opposite question:

> One of the intriguing aspects about forcible sexual assault is the question of symptom choice. *Why does sexuality become the mode of expressing power and anger and of discharging tension and frustration?*[104]

They then point out that the behavior of men who rape is multidetermined by "genetic defects, constitutional vulnerabilities, parental deprivations, pathogenic family patterns, social pathology and developmental traumas,"[105] adding that "forcible, repetitive sexual assault can be understood to be more a result of internal psychological determinants in the offender, than external, situational factors in his environment."[106]

The latter point need not be questioned. The very multiplicity of etiological factors mentioned does indeed give a clear indication of the complex clinical picture and the theoretical apparatus with which the authors respond. On the other hand, the terms are broad enough and the etiological factors universal enough to explain or include just about everything—and also to escape that puzzled "*Why does sexuality become...?*" Certainly the unique case history is important and multidetermined, but so long as the nonrational and irreducible archetypal confluence of sexuality and aggressive power is not recognized as an a priori "just so," one can assume that theorists will continue to derive one principle from the other in support of their favored position. These favored positions are children of their times—sexuality to the Victorian late 19th century, power to the present day influenced as it is by feminism and a broader sociological consciousness.

The recurrence of the contrast between sexuality and power in this context results from a simple laying side by side of the two studies. Presented are two fundamentally conflicting positions brought to bear on the problem of rape by independent investigators. As has been seen, however, the clinical phenomenology approached by the respective authors is the same. One noteworthy aspect of the Groth-Birnbaum study is the female coauthorship of H. Jean Birnbaum as well as the cooperation with Ann Wolbert Burgess and Lynda Lytle Holmstrom, whose intelligent feminist sympathies are well respected.

In spite of the above observations, no simple negation is here intended. The basic theoretical shift toward power in Groth and Birnbaum and other contemporary writers constitutes an historically important and much needed compensation for the fading dominant attitude—supported by classical psychoanalysis—of rape as the product of repressed or uncontrollable sexual passion. One need but recall the 1954 Rorschach study by Abrahamsen, referred to at the beginning of this chapter, to emphasize this point. Especially through studies such as Groth and Birnbaum's, rape seems finally to be recognized as *a problem for men.*

Typical Emotions and Sexual Dysfunction

Groth and Birnbaum report of rapists that "in no case have we ever found that rape was the first sex experience" and also that within their sample all had access to consenting sexual outlets at the time of the rape, and in fact one-third were married.[107] "For the most part, offenders report finding little if any sexual satisfaction in the act of rape."[108] "Subjective emotional distress in the form of anxiety, rage, depression and the like is more closely correlated with the psychological experience of rape than is sexual gratification."[109]

In addition to the limited emotional satisfaction in the rape experience, the assailant may be quite unable to perform physically. Sexual dysfunction, including impotence and premature or retarded ejaculation, is commonplace, occurring in one-third of the cases. What is more, "such dysfunction appears specific to the assault," while presenting no unusual problem in the balance of the man's sexual life.[110] Retarded ejaculation is extraordinarily frequent among rapists as compared to this dysfunction in the general population[111] (another reason why lack of sperm in the alleged victim's vagina does not preclude the possibility that she was indeed raped). The authors allude to a number of auxiliary studies, one of which reports "the presence of one or more negative emotions (hostility, guilt, anger) in conflict with the patient's sexual intent as an underlying factor of impotence," while a second study "related retarded ejaculation to rage . . . instantly mobilized by any threat to the rapist's concept of himself as a man."[112] Generally in psychiatric literature sexual dysfunction as a whole is correlated with psychological mood states of anxiety, depression and anger as well as with conflicts regarding sex—viewed as negative or dirty, as dangerous, etc. These same factors are prominent characteristics of rapists.

The subjects of the studies thus far examined are rapists seen in high-security clinical situations and hence represent an extreme. By far the most rapes go unreported, few of those reported result in arrests and far fewer still result in commitment. Treatment is arduous and "cure" difficult to gauge owing to the impossibility of accurately measuring recidivism. The four authors of the Massachusetts study close their paper with the disquieting statement: "The lifelong pathological relationships with women seen in these three groups of rapists give no reason to believe that a prison sentence will make them less dangerous."[113] (By "prison" here is meant the security medical installation.)

Any possibility of psychological development depends on a person's ability in one way or another to *reflect*. Jung describes reflection as "the cultural instinct *par excellence*" and mentions "ethical conduct" as one of the fruits of this activity.[114] Precisely the inability to reflect stands out as characteristic of the sexual offender; as Groth and Birnbaum observe, "He tends not to be introspective and exhibits little capacity for self-observation."[115] The rapist is emotionally impoverished, overwhelmed with a sense of purposelessness, ill at ease with tender feelings, has a strong system of denial, and is quite incapable of delaying gratification. The rapist is in the grip of psychic forces much greater than himself, as one reports:

> I felt I had to go out and do it. I realized that sooner or later I'd get caught. I realized this would jeopardize my marriage, my job, my freedom, yet I just had to go out and do it, as if some force deep inside me was controlling me.[116]

5

The Archetypal Background of Rape

Fear of the Feminine

In the wake of the preceding chapter, it may appear as if the responsibility for rape has once more been left on the doorstep of a particular group of men, but this is hardly the case. Rather, the extremes of a general problem are represented by clinically observed rapists. A man may begin to gather the problems of rape into himself by imagining, if not recognizing, those compulsive, unreflective, instinctually driven contents of his own psyche which possess so little amenability to "treatment."

No doubt many will revolt at the very idea of such trifling. But what if the unconscious were to set before the inner eye just such a frenetic, emotionally charged image? One young man dreamt:

> A young man has been killed by the black panther, but his mother, a big fat white woman, escapes. Earlier in the night I see a homosexual murderer who has slashed up his entire body with a knife and also admitted that he had "torn off the heads of young girls." And he meant that quite literally!

The dreamer's personality was in no clinical sense pathological—not criminal, neither suicidal nor threatened with a psychosis. In whatever way it may offend cherished notions of "health" or "progress," the presence of such contents in the psyche is completely commonplace, and furthermore—aside from the work of making such things conscious—there is simply nothing to be done about it.

The impulse to destruction, whether in sexual assault or in general, is an irreducible psychological given. Jung has spoken of the need to become "more conscious of the inflexible universal laws that govern even the wildest and the most wanton fantasy."[117] Any individuation process or thorough analytical treatment which fails to face up to even the analysand's most wanton fantasies may well pass by the opportunity of contacting that dynamism of psychic energy which carries the entire process. The sobering facts of the personal and collective shadow are an essential but by no means exclusive realization resulting from the exploration, as will be seen. A crucial qualifying consideration, of course, is the relative degree to which the perverse behavior, obsessive ideation or powerful dream material spontaneously presses upon the analysand, for nothing is gained by the pursuit of extraneous or unconstellated material.

The stark ugliness and destructiveness of actual rape has been sufficiently emphasized. Remaining is an exploration of what psychological meaning the raw deed, but more centrally the raw material, of rape in fantasy or in dreams carries in the psychic process. A basic assumption here is that any fantasy pattern so ubiquitous and so emotionally charged, as deeply rooted in the instinct of sexuality, power and aggression, and as intimately involved in the relationship between masculine and feminine as is rape, possesses immense importance when it appears in psychotherapy. To repeat, hidden in this *prima materia* may be precisely that dynamism driving the individuation process.

Rape and sexuality itself issue from mysterious, instinctive depths which yet carry a divine spark tending upward. The Western world's dominant but fading Christian morality has successfully denied and repressed from consciousness sexuality's natural affinity with spirit, but scarcely destroyed the archetypal fact. Rape, however crudely perpetrated, is one avenue within the psyche by which the numinous aspect of the denied may return. In *The Symbolic Quest*, Edward C. Whitmont points out (quoting Linda Fierz-David):

> In pre-Christian mythological tradition we quite frequently find that the sexual customs and images serve to express central religious mysteries.... "The experience of the mysteries touches in a decisive fashion the depth of sexuality in which the divine and the animal, the holy and the obscene, are inseparably united ... there it is balanced as on a razor's edge whether the most sublime may be reduced to the most base.... In the higher initiation of the mature person the goal is the mysterious union of the human soul with the divine spirit—a 'holy marriage' which is meant to make him the 'twice-born' one and to lead him toward immortality."[118]

The present study began with "the base" and seeks to remain closely mindful of it. Dealing with rape analytically may indeed be a "razor's edge" situation, depending on how closely the patient's actual behavior approximates or has included sexual assault. The moral strength and capacity for reflection play a decisive role in withstanding and following a psychic transformation. The authors of the Massachusetts study referred to above speak of "a decompensation approaching psychotic proportions in men who have been able to deal with their intense rage toward women in relatively successful ways."[119] They go on to question how the aggressive rage itself appears to be "both the result of a splitting of the mother ambivalence and also a defense against the experience of helplessness they feel in all object relationships, but with particular intensity toward women."[120] Any discussion of the individuation process need begin with the original matrix. Therefore, with the fear and anger of the rapist ever in mind, attention may now turn to the unconscious and the dread of the feminine.

Blood is the origin as well as the negation of all life—the hue of birth, the stain of slaughter, a liquid rose of mysterious humors. By the moment of birth every particle of the child's body has been circulated with gentle pulsations through the heart, lungs, the deepest capillary fabric of the mother. Blood is an abyss in itself—the lava flow, the flood, the ocean up and walking around. A genuine sense of primal awe accompanied one analysand's memory from early childhood—one person's intuition and image of a completely collective phenomenon:

> Our sprawling garden had one small cottage in it where a young pregnant woman lived alone as her husband was off to the war. Past the trees and the plum thicket, aged and cheaply acquired horses were slaughtered as food for the mink which were raised on the neighboring farm.
>
> "I wonder how she felt," mused my mother in telling the story, "amidst morning sickness and discomfort, to have rivulets from the spring thaw carry the blood of the horses down the hill, and to have those pools formed around the house be stained with blood?"

Here, as is so typically the case, a fantasy surrounding the personal mother inclines toward the impersonal, the undefinable, the "mother" as an archetypal experience embracing life and death in a unified fluid. Jung well knew this fact and discusses its significance for regression:

> It must be remembered that the "mother" is really an imago, a psychic image merely, which has in it a number of different but very important unconscious contents. The "mother," as the first incarnation of the anima archetype, personifies in fact the whole unconscious. Hence the regression leads back only apparently to the mother; in reality she is the gateway into the unconscious, into the "realm of the Mothers." . . . For regression, if left undisturbed, does not stop short at the "mother" but goes back beyond her to the prenatal realm of the "Eternal Feminine," to the immemorial world of archetypal possibilities where "thronged round with images of all creation," slumbers the "divine child," patiently awaiting his conscious realization.[121]

Jung's own insight was gained through no especially easy process of reflection, rather through his own horrific plunge into the blood of this "mother."[122]

Inward confrontation has ever and always been avoided by the vast majority of men. Of course there are many good reasons for this, not least the possibility of being swamped into madness. But the resort to brute force as in rape, or even the overly transcendent elaborations of the intellectual, betrays a deep fear and resentment regarding women and the unconscious. As Karen Horney questioned already in 1932:

> Is it not really remarkable (we ask ourselves in amazement) when one considers the overwhelming mass of this transparent material, that so little recognition and attention are paid to the fact of men's secret dread of women? The man on his side has in the first place very obvious strategic reasons for keeping his dread quiet. But he tries by every means to deny it even to himself. . . . We may conjecture that even his glorification of women has its source not only in the cravings of love, but also in his desire to give the lie to his dread.[123]

Depreciation and loathing of woman, her body and by extension the feminine, has been expressed repeatedly by our intellectual and psychological forefathers, though not always in the most intellectual fashion. Aristotle emphasized how "the female does not contribute semen to generation" and that male semen is a more highly refined form of blood than the female menses;[124] Tertullian exclaimed, "Woman! You are the gateway of the devil. . . . Because of you the Son of God had to die," and he described woman as "a temple built over a sewer"; St. Augustine disgustedly reflects upon the proximity of sexual and excretory organs with the famous phrase "*Inter faeces et urinum nascimur*" (between shit and piss are we born); Linnaeus avoided as "abominable" the study of female sex organs; and the French physician des Laurens asks in despair, "How can this divine animal, full of reason and judgement, which we call man, be attracted by these obscene parts of woman, defiled with juices and located shamefully at the lowest part of the trunk?"[125] The year 1900 saw the publication of *Uber das Physiologische Schwachsinn des Weibes* by J. P. Moebius which elaborates a doctrine of female inferiority. Again, the influential misogynist Otto Weininger confidently dubbed women "soulless" and mentally inferior, but found himself sufficiently susceptible to a pathological sentimentality to kill himself in Beethoven's house in 1903 at the age of a mere 23.[126]

This book opened with the dream of the fervent Greek man in a tragic attempt to transcend his own shadow; inevitably, it seems, the saint and the whoremonger join hands in the dark, a darkness where an entire spectrum of goddesses surround a spinning wheel of Fate or hold Kali's rosary of human skulls. The feminine element denigrated and repressed takes on an ever more explosive counterposition in the unconscious. The shadow blends into the same unconscious background. The rapist in his lack of reflection and possessing no image of his psychic hinterground becomes the very image of the shadow—the son and exponent of the instinctive unconscious. His ignorance of that with which he is dealing is suggested by an early 18th-century story:

> Three youths raped a beautiful lady; after the crime she says to them: "You imagine that you have caught a splendid game . . . I will show you who I am." Thereupon she lifts her skirts and they perceive, under her clothes, a stinking, repulsive carcass.[127]

This corresponds to the traditional German image of *Frau Welt* who, beautiful, bounteous and inviting, turns round to reveal a morbid back alive with worms, toads and snakes.

The often described rift in the mother image of the rapist and his ambivalence toward her, however exacerbated, is scarcely characteristic of the rapist alone. And it is certainly not reducible to the personal mother or to the mother and wife alone. Such a polarity rests in all men upon an archetypal basis. In one California study rapists asked to describe the kind of victim they "preferred" responded by portraying "the American dream ideal—a nice, friendly, young, pretty, middle-class, white female," and most wanting "a completely passive victim."[128] They imagined they would catch a "splendid game," while remaining completely unconscious of the negative, malignant, dark side of the feminine. This is understandably the case, for the task of confronting the instinctual background would cut to the quick the rapist's immense feeling of inadequacy, his castration anxiety and his fear of madness.

The act of rape itself is an attempt to shore up phallic pride and the weakness of an uninitiated ego entrapped in a phallic self-love with little else to fall back on. With an eye to love and power, Karen Horney says it succinctly:

> In sexual life itself we see how the simple craving of love which drives men to women is often overshadowed by their own overwhelming inner compulsion to prove their manhood over again and again to themselves and others. A man of this type in its more extreme form has therefore one interest only: to conquer. . . . We find a remarkable mixture of this narcissistic over-compensation and of surviving anxiety in those men who while wanting to make conquests, are very indignant with a woman who takes their intentions too seriously, or who cherish a lifelong gratitude to her if she spares them any further proof of their manhood.[129]

One widespread fantasy of the threatening female is that of the *vagina dentata*. From the numerous tales reproduced in Wolfgang Lederer's *Fear of Women*, in the chapter "A Snapping of Teeth," the following is an especially appropriate image of the rapist's dilemma:

> There was a Rakshaa's (demon's) daughter who had sharp teeth in her vagina. When she saw a man, she would turn into a pretty girl, seduce him, cut off his penis, eat it herself and throw the rest of his body to her tigers. One day she met seven brothers in the jungle and married the eldest so that she could sleep with all of them. After some

time she took the eldest boy to where the tigers lived, made him lie with her, cut off his penis, and gave his body to the tigers. In the same way she killed the six brothers until only the youngest was left. When his turn came, the gods who helped him, sent him a dream: "If you go with the girl," said the god, "make an iron tube, put it into her vagina and break her teeth." This the boy did.[130]

Borne in mind, as a compensation to any reaction which would make this merely a charming tale from the East, may be the "trademark" of Alberto de Salvo, the Boston Strangler—a broomstick rammed into the vagina of his murdered victims.

With such a pervasive fear of the threatening female, the common sexual dysfunction of the rapist is not so surprising. Of particular note is the way in which this problem is situationally specific. Rape is a highly stressful and ambivalent act. The woman carries the simultaneous projection of the desired and the hated, the object of impulses to possess as in robbery and to destroy as in assault. In the rapist's fantasy the woman may be alluring, yet secretly an ally of the instinctual tigers which threaten to consume the assailant, and *have* consumed him as he descends on his prey. Before passing on to finer differentiations of these basic dynamics, let us look at a modern myth, a myth of a rapist as the toy of archetypal forces, a myth the more striking for its very reality.

Charles Manson: Son of the Terrible Mother

Charles Manson, famous as overlord of "the family" that perpetrated the Tate-LaBianca murders in California in 1969, provides a quintessential example of a person in the grip of an archetype.

Rapist, thief, drug dealer and murderer, Manson proclaimed himself Christ and elaborated an ideology of anarchic millennialism, an eschatology of impending doom. Central to this was the concept of "The Hole": "Inside this mystic Hole in Death Valley, Manson and his family would live and dwell while the blacks and whites in the cities would fight to a bloody end."[131] He taught, furthermore, that his family's work would be to bring "seven holes on the seven planes into alignment" within the Hole which would enable them "to squirt through to the other side of the universe."[132] Progressive accretions to this fantasy included his machete and machine gun equipped dune-buggies as the horses of the Apocalypse with "breast-plates of fire," the Beatles as the "four angels" who would destroy a third of mankind, and Manson's "scriptural basis for announcing that the Beatles were destined to have a fifth member or 'angel'—the angel of the bottomless pit"[133] (Manson himself, of course).

As there was need of a military wing, motorcycle gangs were

lured as allies, with the perpetual sexual availability of Manson's
young female followers playing no small part in the transaction.
Four members of a cycle group called "Satan's Slaves" brought with
them an additional influence: they were linked with an occult group
led by a woman believed by them to be an incarnation of Circe, the
goddess who magically turned the men of Odysseus to swine. The
group celebrated seaside orgies at new and full moon which included the blood sacrifice of black dogs, black cats, black roosters
and probably also goats.[134] The members were anointed and blood
was drunk as a sacrament. There are also numerous indications that
members of Manson's family participated in the filmed sacrificial
murders of young female victims. "As violence overwhelmed him,
Manson would be seen jumping around . . . slashing and jabbing the
air with the sword," one witness recalls.[135] Manson also gave lessons
on knife throwing, throat slitting and skull boiling.

> Charlie had an old sixteen-inch army surplus machete and he was the
> only one who could throw it. . . . He used to put girls up against the
> haystack and see how close he could throw the machete to them.
>
> In his universe, women had no soul. They were to be slaves of Man.
>
> The girls were required instantly to submit to the men Manson
> stated to be on the grope list. Anytime, anywhere. The girls suppos-
> edly were not allowed to ask for sex but had to wait. . . .
>
> Manson is known to blame women for the institution of capital
> punishment, for jails, and for practically all repression.
>
> "We live in a woman's thought, this world is hers. But men were
> meant to be above, on top of women."
>
> He hated women. "I am a mechanical boy, I am my mother's boy,"
> went one of his songs.[136]

The striking line, "We live in a woman's thought," is the utterance
of a child of the Great Mother, the pet of Circe, one less a personality than the personification of an archetype. The use of threats and
brute force in dominating his band of teenage girls concomitant with
the fear of jails and repression by women displays as well the
paranoid ambivalence of this rapist and murderer.

The Christian West has no major, traditional representation of
the terrible aspect of the archetypal feminine, as India, for example,
has in the Hindu goddess Kali. This "skull-bedecked mistress of the
boneyard" appears in numerous animal forms including lion and
tiger, besides her black or red anthropomorphic form.[137] She commonly appears standing on a boat adrift in a sea of blood. Lederer
provides a vivid sense of her nature:

> She is the fury of growth that fights for every inch of earth and air,
> the dumb fury of the creature, the fury of sexual heat and the urge to
> conception, the implacable drive for ever new fertility that whips the
> creatures onward through life and death.[138]

The Archetype of the Masculine

The archetype of the masculine is a vast, polar psychic organ with its own tendencies toward exclusivity. One of the clearer characterizations of the masculine spirit is made by Mircea Eliade in his discussion of "The Sky and Sky Gods": "The most popular prayer in the world is addressed to 'Our Father who art in Heaven.' It is possible that man's earliest prayers were addressed to the same heavenly father."[140]

Eliade continues by citing instances of the universal experience of the divinity of the heavenly spirit in early cultures. Qualities which he finds attributed to this heavenly spirit include "the Most High," "the shining," "force," "law," "sovereignty," "storm," "great," "luminous," "omniscient," etc. In most cultures archetypal images of the extreme aerial pole of the archetype present themselves, and reside, high in the sphere of the collective psyche. Another quality which Eliade sees as recurrent is the *aloof* nature of the Most High. This underscores the polar extreme of this type of figure; the flaming palace of Yahweh in *The Book of Enoch,* Zeus on Olympus, Atum Ra, the fiery rings of Anaximander, or simply the Sun provide illustrious examples. The relativity of this spiritual pole—or as Eliade terms it, the "specialization" of the masculine spirit—to earth, to the feminine, to human conditions, is equally ubiquitous:

> The "specialization" of sky gods into gods of hurricanes and of rain, and also the stress on their fertility powers, is largely explained by the passive nature of sky divinities, and their tendency to give place to other hierophanes that are more concrete, more clearly personal, more directly involved in the daily life of man. This fate results largely from the transcendence of the sky and man's ever increasing "thirst for the concrete."[141]

Again Eliade returns to the same theme:

> The rain—the storm god's "sowing"—fits in with the hierophany of the waters, which are the most important sphere the moon dominates. Everything connected with fecundity belongs, more or less directly, to the immense orbit of the Moon—Waters—Woman—Earth. Sky divinities became firmly bound up with these prehistoric patterns, and have remained there, either assimilating them into their own personalities, or becoming part of them.[142]

Through the emphasis provided by this material upon the transcendent nature of the archetype in its aerial extreme, the way is paved for an appreciation of the reciprocally deep instinctual and chthonic pole of the archetypal masculine. By alluding to Eliade's discussion of sky gods and following the tendency for them to be replaced by others "more concrete, more clearly personal, more

directly involved in the daily life of man," one is metaphorically
descending along the "axis" of the archetype to that sublunary and
earthly level in which the power and sovereignty of the masculine
grows ever more relative to the instinctual power and material fact
of the Earth Goddess. Here is where matter and energy, masculine
and feminine, spirit and instinct battle in that dynamic oneness
which is the daily life of man. And here too is where the mundane
act of rape takes the stage—a physical and a psychological event in
the center of a material and spiritual world.

One may well recall Hesiod's comparison of the height of heaven
to the depth of Tartaros. In the *Theogony* it was precisely the establishment of the sovereignty of Zeus which threw Hades and the
Underworld into such abysmal relief. In order to appreciate psychologically the drive for the establishment of power so characteristic of
many men and particularly of the rapist, the full range of the
archetype need be borne in mind. The center of gravity is as ter-
restrial as everyday life, and the vicissitudes of masculine identity,
integrity and development are relative to the feminine at every turn.
This relativity to the feminine appears increasingly more pronounced with the descent already imagined.

Particular attention to the chthonic pole of the archetype has
been paid by Erich Neumann. In describing the origins of consciousness he begins with a completely androgynous, primal matrix—the
uroboros—from which consciousness emerges. This profoundly "maternal" representation of the collective unconscious is further conceived as a pair of broadly defined World Parents. Of these, the
"patriarchal uroboros" is primarily related by Neumann to the archetypal background of sovereignty and law which lends compelling
power to the tenets of the prevailing culture upon the individual. He
points out, however, that standing in contrast to this ordering principle of social and individual consciousness is its own shadow, or
"negative" pole, lying deep in the original matrix of the unconscious,
as far beneath the earth as its "positive" pole stands above. This
"Terrible Male," still in close contact with the mother, is described
by Neumann in the following way:

> The devouring darkness . . . can . . . appear just as easily in the mascu-
> line form of a monster like Set or the Fenris Wolf.
> . . . In these figures the accent falls primarily on the devouring
> forces, i.e., the uterine cave. Even when they later appear in the
> patriarchate as genuine Terrible Father figures, e.g., Cronos or Mol-
> och, their uroboric character is transparent so long as the symbolism
> of eating is in the foreground and hence their propinquity to the
> Great Mother.
> *Similarly, the phallic-chthonic earth and sea divinities are . . . simply
> satellites of the Great Mother.*[143]

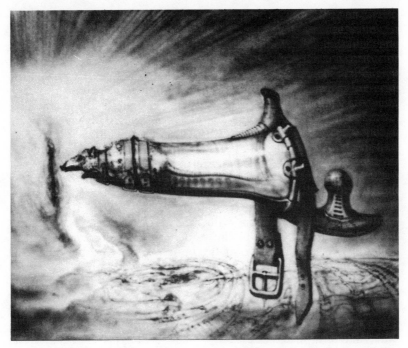

"Rattenbild," a modern fantasy of the Terrible Male, by Swiss artist
H.R. Giger.—From *Necronomicon.*

To the degree that the ego differentiates itself from the "maternal"
unconscious it begins to cast shadow, i.e., to gradually experience the
destructive side of the Great Mother as something masculine as well.

The formation of ego and shadow in personal psychology is
played out upon the same separation and polarization of the archetypal masculine into aerial and underworld as mythologically described. Neumann describes the two powerful extremes with which
the ego is confronted, the following passage elaborating on one in
particular:

> The Terrible Father appears to the hero [ego] in two transpersonal
> figures: as the phallic Earth Father and the frightening Spirit Father.
> The Earth Father, lord of all chthonic forces, belongs psychologically
> to the realm of the Great Mother. He manifests himself most com-
> monly as the overwhelming aggressiveness of phallic instinct or as a
> destructive monster. But whenever the ego is overwhelmed by the
> sexual, aggressive, or power instincts of the male, or by any other
> form of instinct, we can see the dominance of the Great Mother. For

she is the instinctual ruler of the unconscious, mistress of animals, and the phallic Terrible Father is only her satellite, not a masculine princi-ple of equal weight.[144]

With this in mind, recall the case of Charles Manson. Already considered as a child of the Terrible Mother, he may be viewed too as a child of the "phallic Earth Father, lord of all chthonic forces." Manson's own frantic sovereignty, his phallic power (he was said to have had sexual intercourse four to five times daily over several years), his claims of being the Christ combined with his eschatologi-cal doctrine of "The Hole" are all qualities characteristic of the negative aspect of the masculine spirit.

Manson's behavior may be imagined as inspired by Pan, by Dionysos or Hades, or again in terms of Jung's description of the Mana personality in its negative aspect. His own fantasy makes it reasonable to consider him with reference to Christ. Immediately evident is that in contrast to Christ, the Son of the Heavenly Father, Manson is decidedly a son of the underworldly Terrible Father—a shadow image of the perfect, innocent and ascetic Christ. As Christ went to prepare a place in Paradise, so Manson prepared his follow-ers to descend into the Hole; where Christ stated, "I and the Father are One," Manson said, "We live in a woman's thought" and "I am my mother's boy." The point here is the possibility of identification with, and complete possession by, the archetype of the spirit at either of its poles. Manson's fantasy of the seven holes and those seven mysterious planes beneath the Earth which, aligned, would allow passage to the other side of the universe, is an excellent illustration of a psyche unconsciously seeking its opposite (i.e., enan-tiodromia).

Pristine archetypal material such as this, elaborated in a context apocalyptic in scope, is the hallmark of one possessed by the spirit. An amplification not only of the seven-fold abyss, but also of the full polarity of the spirit of God stretching from the height of heaven to the nethermost depths appears in a powerful document of some of the earliest constellations of the Messiah in Judaism. In *The Book of Enoch*, the prophet is swept up to a celestial temple of crystal and fire—to which even the cherubs and angels of Yahweh are denied entrance—before he views the horrific netherworldy pole of the Almighty. The sequence of visions includes the chambers of all the winds, the foundations and cornerstone of the earth, and then the deep abyss:

...and what I saw there was horrible fire pillars beyond number in the center of the abyss toward the height and toward the depth, and seven burning stars, like great burning mountains, like spirits which besought me.

And the angel said, "This is the place where heaven and earth terminate. The seven stars are held because of their guilt until the year of the mystery. *Here stand the angels who have connected themselves with women.*"

And I saw there something horrible, I saw neither heaven or a firmly founded earth, but a place chaotic and horrible: stars which have transgressed the commandment of God, bound for 10,000 ages.[145]

The spiritual drama of Enoch began with a number of heavenly angels falling in love with the daughters of earth, a legend also mentioned in the sixth chapter of Genesis. Extremely impressive is the fierce antagonism between the spirit of God the Father and the feminine—as well as His own lower pole—in this profoundly archetypal constellation. These images of the cosmic dynamism created between the aerial sovereign and the seven burning star/mountain/spirits of the abyss appeared to an unknown prophet during a time of the brutal persecution of his people in approximately 120 B.C.

This material illustrates the manner in which *human psychological experience* (here that of an anonymous prophet under the pseudonym of Enoch) takes place in an intermediary realm, at the archetypal center of gravity. The sustained polarity is connected with the idea of "ages," i.e., duration in time, yet simultaneously the experience of the *unity* of the spiritual spectrum embraces timelessness, apocalypse and—following Enoch's vision of Paradise later in the book—a psychic restoration of an "earlier state of things."

The Book of Enoch represents a grand collective vision, but considered in terms of personal psychology it illuminates not only the case of Charles Manson but also the depth psychology of the typical rapist. The Massachusetts study described "a decompensation approaching psychotic proportions in men who have been able to deal with their intense rage toward women in relatively successful ways" (above, page 55). This amounts to precisely that type of unearthly confrontation not with women alone, but with *"their intense rage toward women."* In light of the current of both lay and scientific misogyny seen historically and in case histories, as well as in the assembled mythological material, an important insight emerges: the raping rage toward the feminine cannot be explained reductively in terms of personalistic mothers or ambivalent wives but proves to be an essential characteristic of the archetype of the masculine itself—an irreducible, a priori factor. The answer is not the virgin, but the mad unicorn! A man has to not only reappraise his attitude toward the feminine, but also, and more fundamentally, grapple with his personal identity as a man within the archetypal sphere of the Father.

Characteristic of the archetype of the masculine spirit, and contrasting with the Great Mother in whom all individuals are as sprouting and perishing plants, is the quality of *hierarchy*. In the cosmological speculation of Mithraism and Gnosticism as well as in the mythology of shamanism, the upward and downward mobility of the spirit is commonly imagined or enacted up or down through seven cosmic levels, corresponding to planets, personified as Archons, etc. Like Manson's band "squirting through to the other side of the universe" is the passage from pole to pole, above and below, along the axis of the psychic universe. This is among the most fundamental of archetypal ideas, appearing in imagery of the Cosmic Tree such as the Norse Yggdrasil or the Siberian shaman's notched pole, as well as the axis of pyramid and ziggurat, Jacob's ladder, the chakra system of yoga, the spinal mythology of the Osiris Djed Festival, etc. The polarity of the archetype is however better imaged in high and low personifications; for example, Yahweh/Satan, Christ/Antichrist, Zeus/Hades (Zeus Chthonius), Asgard/Hel, etc. Other images, with a highly differentiated emphasis on the creative aspect, are the incarnations of Vishnu, from fish, tortoise, boar, man-lion and dwarf on to the apocalyptic Kalki.

Returning more specifically to the question of rape, a useful schema appears in the discussion by Emma Jung of the animus or masculine spirit as manifesting power, deed, word and meaning:

> With these four expressions, which are meant to reproduce the Greek *logos*, the quintessence of the masculine principle does indeed seem to be expressed. At the same time, we find in them a progressive sequence, each stage having its representative in life as well as in the development of the animus. Power corresponds very well to the first stage, the deed follows, then the word and finally, as the last stage, meaning. *One might better say instead of power, directed power, that is will, because mere power is not yet human, nor is it spiritual.*[146]

In the psychology of men who rape, though not them alone, the manifestation of the masculine quite clearly corresponds to the first and most rudimentary stage, that of directed power.

Of course it must be borne in mind that such sequential descriptions of an archetypal principle refer to the role of the archetype in the soul at a certain stage of the individuation process, and do not denote "stages" of the Logos as a transcendental principle. Indeed, even in the psychology of a very mature personality all the various experiential levels of the masculine remain. This is the hallmark of a balanced relationship with the archetype, whereas identification with either extreme of the spectrum brings a potentially catastrophic inflation and loss of soul. The human tragedy of Charles Manson's enthrallment in the underwordly vortex of the archetype is one manifest example.

In our Western Christian tradition men have yearned for an experience of the spirit, perhaps the most natural impulse of the religious instinct. But our religious history has recorded no small number of instances in which a relationship with the Almighty has given way to a total identification with the dark side of spirit, with results no less obscene, no less catastrophic than the legacy of Charles Manson. Shadow too is omnipresent! No less destructive potential exists in the eccentricity of a world-negating aerial mysticism than in an equally unconscious surrender to the whirlpool of "The Hole." One need only mention in this regard the libertinism of certain Gnostic sects that engaged in mystical orgies, the "spiritual integrity" of whose doctrines were aided by abortion and infanticide; or again, the sexual license and psychopathic shadow phenomena of numerous millennialist visionaries in the late Middle Ages; or finally, the horrors of torture and murder perpetrated against the women of Europe in the late 15th century by Heinrich Kramer, James Sprenger and their accomplices with the pious blessing of Pope Innocence VIII.[147]

6

The Rape Fantasy and Individuation

Introduction

Thus far, rape has been considered as a crime, as a feminist and a sociological issue, and also from the perspective of the victim of sexual assault. An attempt has been made in examining the various theoretical contexts in which the problem of rape has appeared to reflect upon their respective assumptions, strengths or inadequacies. In Krafft-Ebing's old medical and physiological view a typically 19th-century chauvinism and biological reductionism proved as unacceptable as his early regard for psychic dynamics in their own right proved instructive.

However much an allegiance to an ultimately physiological basis for psychic events was maintained by Freud and his followers, their exploration of the meaning of sexuality beyond mere reproduction— as a factor intimately bound up with the full range of psychic phenomena—has been recognized as a major contribution. Exaggerated of course is the contention of orthodox psychoanalysis that higher psychic functions, mental and spiritual factors spring merely from the "sublimation" of crude sexual instincts. The view that the aerial pole of the archetype of masculine spirit is derived through sublimation is the logical product of a concretistic and overly reductive attitude. The equally logical dilemma of this one-sided perspective has already been seen in Freud's paper "Beyond the Pleasure Principle" where the problem of individual destiny, i.e., Thanatos, arises to meet Eros. This is the problem between "ego instincts" and sexual instincts. The initial irony of Freud's equation of Thanatos with "ego instincts" is explained by recognizing that the ego's drive toward its own life is simultaneously its drive toward an individually unique death. Both concepts denote the differentiation of the individual from the collective common denominator of sex and species. Freud's one-sided allegiance to sexuality naturally made the ego's demands for its own integrity a problematic factor. Adler's psychology of the individual with its almost exclusive emphasis on the ego and on power represents the contrasting position. The two mutually compensatory positions however seek to describe one psychological reality, which—and this is a crucial fact—requires more than a mere scientific understanding. One may recall Freud's glimpse from the threshold of rationalism of "quite a different region" (page 37) with its mythical rather than scientific hypotheses. As has been seen, clinical studies even now display their reserve, siding either with sexuality or power.

The present psychological perspective views the impulse behind concrete rape and the intrapsychic fantasy of rape as the dynamic drive of the individuation process, regardless of how crude or concrete the attempt or the fantasy may be. This dynamic instinctual/spiritual drive carries within it sexuality, power and an indeterminable number of other components—including an equally irreducible religious instinct. As Jung has pointed out:

> If psychology remains for us only a science, we do not penetrate into life—we merely serve the absolute aim of science. It leads us, certainly, to a knowledge of the objective situation, but it always opposes every other aim but its own. . . . It shrinks from the step which takes it out of itself and which denies its universal validity, since from the standpoint of the intellect everything else is *nothing but fantasy*.[148]

Regarding the importance of fantasy, he continues:

> How fantasy is assessed by psychology, so long as this remains merely science, is illustrated by the well-known views of Freud and Adler. . . . Freud's is a psychology of instinct, Adler's an ego-psychology. Instinct is an impersonal biological phenomenon. A psychology founded on instinct must by its very nature neglect the ego, since the ego owes its existence to the *principium individuationis*, i.e., to individual differentiation, whose isolated character removes it from the realm of general biological phenomena.[149]

And finally, in the context of discussing "negative attempts to free the individuality"—of which rape certainly is an example—Jung remarks:

> Highly remarkable [is the] fact, which any unprejudiced observer is bound to corroborate, . . . that Freud's *"infantile eroticism"* and Adler's *"power drive"* are one and the same thing*, regardless of the clash of opinion between the two schools. It is simply a fragment of uncontrolled, and at first uncontrollable, primordial instinct that comes to light. . . . The archaic fantasy-forms that gradually reach the surface of consciousness are only a further proof of this.[150]

One perfect example of the type of "archaic fantasy-forms" which stand behind consciousness is the androgyne of Plato's *Symposium* which, as has been seen, Freud could not accept. Arising at the vanishing-point of rational comprehension, images such as this are not simply primitive, infantile or regressive illusions, as Freud believed, but are living symbols in the full sense of the term. They preclude further scientific penetration, and one *is* indeed left with a myth and not a scientific explanation, but also with a more comprehensive view of the reality of the psyche. To consider rape as a *prima materia* of the individuation process is to view it symbolically as a reflection of an intrapsychic process. The symbol, neither rational nor irrational, involving thinking, feeling, intuition as well as sensation, and formulating an essentially unconscious factor, is the image par excellence of the integrative activity of the psyche.

An essential clarification must be made before proceeding, namely that the bringing of rape into relationship with the individuation process derives not from an exaggerated sympathy for the rapist, but from a sober recognition of the nature of the intrapsychic process. Duly emphasized has been the criminality of concrete rape and the razor's edge between the sacred and the obscene on which the analytical problem of rape is balanced. Important to note also is Jung's sharp contrasting of *passive* fantasy, with its symptomatic actions, and *active* fantasy through which potential symptomatic behavior is precluded by means of reflective, emotional and symbolic psychological work. He stresses how the latter stands or falls depending on the "symbolic attitude of the observing consciousness,"[151] and the manner in which the symbol "must derive equally from the lowest and most primitive levels of the psyche."[152] A comment such as this is read with ease and passed by, but it implies so full a confrontation with the most base and violent aspects of human nature that it is astounding that Jung has been imagined by some as an otherworldly mystic.

The rapist of course lives out his symptomatic actions, simultaneously in the realm of the Great Mother and in the grip of the underworldly pole of the archetype of the masculine—the "Terrible Male." Approached again with the Logos "stages" of Emma Jung, he may be considered a manifestation of the masculine spirit in its most rudimentary form, i.e., power. Further, a recollection of the pronounced incapacity for psychological reflection so characteristic of the hard-core rapist may be useful in effectively banishing any naive optimism which may have crept in amidst the preceding reflections on spirit. It cannot be overemphasized in pursuing the present theme that instinct and spirit ultimately represent poles of one nonrational phenomenon. The mere adoption of a mythical or archetypal view of psychic material does nothing to change the world as it is, but it does provide the perspective appropriate to the psyche's own nature and behavior.

The accent of the most recent works on rape falls on the question of power. Rape is a desperate attempt on the part of the sexual offender to protect and enhance the integrity of the ego. As Jung has pointed out, the ego owes its very existence to the principle of differentiation. It is necessary to expand on this idea. Most simply this is the innate drive within the psyche toward individual consciousness and identity vis-à-vis all collective phenomena without and within. Many mythological figures might be mentioned as personifications of this principle, including Ares, Prometheus, Mercurius, Eros and the Logos son Christ. Appropriate particularly to the theme of rape is Mars in that this figure embodies the brute, warlike and aggressive nature of man standing opposed to, and yet in love with, Aphrodite. Jung states that Mars (Ares) may be considered as "the principle of individuation in the strict sense."[153] This "strict sense" denotes the individuating principle as hot, violent, sulphurous. Mars represents power and anger in rudimentary and concrete form—rapists as "shock troops." Recognizable in the passion of Mars is Emma Jung's characterization of the Logos principle at the stage where it is power alone. Clearly a paradoxical formulation, it denotes discrimination, consciousness and meaning *in potentia*. In discussing the Logos Jung states:

> There is no consciousness without discrimination of opposites. This is the paternal principle, the Logos, which eternally struggles to extricate itself from the primal warmth and primal darkness of the maternal womb; in a word, from unconsciousness. Divine curiosity yearns to be born and does not shrink from conflict, suffering, or sin. Unconsciousness is the primal sin, evil itself, for the Logos. Therefore its first creative act of liberation is matricide.[154]

This observation aligns with what has already been stated of the struggle of the masculine over against the feminine in rape, intent as the masculine is on its own sovereignty. Groth and Birnbaum report of the typical rapist, "Although his cognitive abilities appear intact, his actual behavior appears inconsistent with his rational functioning. Although intellectually competent, he tends to exhibit poor judgment, especially when he is emotionally aroused or under stress."[155] Calling attention to the deficient development of Logos in the rapist sounds well-nigh facetious given his poor judgment. Though it is not so likely to result in actual rape, the extreme of overly developed Logos—an exaggerated intellectualism or one-sided rationalism—also can display a fear and denigration of the feminine.

The Logos at whatever stage of its manifestation struggles eternally to extricate itself from the primal fear of the mother world, and "matricide" takes many a form. In a profound sense rape attempts psychological matricide. But when the mother is too powerfully internal and too deeply unconscious to be confronted as an inner problem, the outer woman falls victim to the concrete assertion of masculine power.

The Longing for Union

The great irony, of course, is that the destructive act of sexual assault is simultaneously an act of union—of Eros. By Eros, however, nothing more elevated is implied here than is meant in viewing unconscious Logos as devouring brute force. For just as unconscious Logos, so too, writes Jung, "an unconscious Eros always expresses itself as will to power."[156]

Clinical evidence of the rapist's undifferentiated Eros need scarcely be introduced. His Eros is rather that of a child, whose organism sleepily or tyrannically flourishes in the maternal embrace. He lacks the ability to relate to women for his Eros is unconsciously bound to the mother, forever impeding his movement into life. As the ego's obsession with its own end is still bound by the species, a tremendous tension filled with the ambivalent fear of life and death escalates—caving in, acting out, or transformation being the options. With this tension of opposites an old question comes to mind, a question already posed by Karen Horney:

> Are love and death more closely bound up with one another for the male than the female? *Does the man feel, side by side with his desire to conquer, a secret longing for extinction in the act of reunion with the woman (mother)?* Is it perhaps this longing which underlies the "death instinct"?[157]

Horney's intuition that love and death do not ultimately oppose one another points again beyond the pleasure principle as well as beyond the ego to a symbolic razor's edge. What intentionality resides in the tension? To what is the union leading? An initial idea is offered by Simone de Beauvoir:

> There is in erotic love a tearing away from self, transport, ecstacy; *suffering also tears through the limits of the ego,* it is transcendence, a paroxysm; pain has always played a great part in orgies; and it is well known that the exquisite and the painful intermesh; a caress can become torture, torment can give pleasure. The embrace leads easily to biting, pinching, scratching; but such behavior is not ordinarily sadisitic; it shows a desire to blend, not to destroy; and the individual who suffers is not seeking rejection and humiliation, but union.[158]

She speaks of actual lovers, but the tension just described is a psychological suffering of a conflict for which the ego has no solution. De Beauvoir rightly emphasizes the manner in which the immersion in aggressive sexual passion overwhelms the ego in an experience of *transcendence,* but what of erotic *hate*—of behavior blatantly sadistic?

Indeed love and hate are not the opposites which the naive mind might suppose, but dynamic qualities within Eros itself. Rather, the abstracting principle of Logos in the higher sense, or "objective interest" as Jung calls it, stands in contrast to love and hate. Eros in its dark and negative aspect hardens into hate, bent on the destruction of its object. A major component in the maintenance of the ego, the emotion of hate is exacerbated and brought to the fore in more desperate efforts for ego defense. James Hillman emphasizes this:

> The frigid river Styx (whose name, "hateful" or "hatred" derives from *stygeo*, "to hate") is the deepest source of the Gods' morality, for on its waters they swear their oaths, implying that hatred plays an essential part in the universal order of things. . . .
> Styx's children are called Zellus (Zeal), Nike (Victory), Bia (Force) and Cratos (Strength). Their mother's cold hatred is converted by them into those implacable traits we have come to accept as virtues.[159]

In the psychology of rape both Eros and Logos (Logos as power in the sense of Emma Jung) function at the archaic level, intermingled in a Stygian current. The zeal, victory, force and strength displayed or intended by the rapist against his victim are all an intimate part of his ego's struggle to maintain control. The isolation springing from this very drive, and the diminishing adaptation of the ego to its origins, eventually brings up that "secret longing for extinction." Whether it be called "transcendence," "*abaissment du niveau mental*," "decompensation" or whatever, the burdened ego tends toward the easiest outlet.

In discussing a case of extreme sadism, Medard Boss describes hating as an existential mode of being in the world, as well as a means of escaping from it. Hatred is seen as a factor in itself, as frigid and remote as the river Styx:

> Each resistance which E. K. met against his only possible form of living and broadening of existence against the self-glorying abuse and the unscrupulous devouring of his surroundings provoked a "terrible hatred" in the patient. His experience of this reaction demonstrates clearly [that] the phenomenon of hate has never been justly dealt with scientifically, if it is only conceived as an act of "intentional interest" (Bretano) or as an "affect" which can "suddenly turn" into other "affects," even into love. No less a part of the real experience of hate is its abstraction to "aggressive drive" (Adler, Freud), which has its analogy in the reduction of love to the "sex-drive." In order to do justice to the reality content of hate, hate must be considered an original, fundamental form of existence.
> In the case of E. K. everything certainly speaks for the fact that he —as a hating person—exists in the world in quite a special way. The outlines and limitations of all concrete shapes just don't become transparent, and these shapes and figures do not manifest beauty and loveliness as is the case in the enthusiasm of the mode of being-in-

love. . . . Moreover his hate drags each concrete factual form into an infernal chaos. He is so alien to all the richness and loveliness of form and shape that it distorts everything into an ugly "deformed" appearance. In the patient's life the entire world is twisted by his hate "to a grotesque and dwarf-like tightness." His hate tries to annihilate the world as well as the patient himself forever, reducing both to dust, *because hate does not only destroy the time and space of the world, just as love overcomes it, but because hate—as does love—reaches beyond the separation into subject and object.*[160]

The patient E. K. had reached the point of binding, beating and slashing his victims. Boss further comments that:

In this drastic way, the love "will to union" of the sadomasochist makes use of the "worldliest of worldly techniques," namely destruction and deformation, to break open the earthly finite barriers of the clod-world, since they could not be overcome and permeated by love in a different way.[161]

In spite of Boss's insistence upon hate as a "fundamental form of existence" he closely correlates hate and love—both are seen as modes of transcending the "finite barriers of the clod-world." This is nothing less than an attempt of the psyche to, in Freud's words, "restore an earlier state of things"—the ego's escape from an intolerable isolation toward some psychological experience of totality.

Of course becoming drunk, drugged or totally overwhelmed by a vicious affect is an escape for the isolated ego. But there is a tremendous difference between breaking the bounds of subject and object in a frenzied assault and patiently withstanding the warring opposites until the transcendent function, the conflict-reconciling symbol, manifests. Thus the crucial question for a psychotherapy concerned with the transformation of the personality is one of reflective containment. Although the most intense instincts demand and generally enforce concrete gratification, can destructive behavior be avoided, can the instinct be borne without psychosis or suicide? The regressive process may indeed be a dangerous one, but only through a sober confrontation with one's own psychology can the drives which would be taken so literally and acted out so concretely be transformed into some consciousness of the greater wholeness of the personality.

Given this essential containment, and considering the intimate relation of dynamic inner events to one's identity beyond mere egohood, to teleological questions and to ultimate meaning, the dreams and fantasies arising in analysis are rightfully considered also with regard to the *religious* instinct. Though it may appear a cruel jest to bring rape and sexual assault into relation with the religious instinct, the essential connection between the sacred and the obscene, as noted by Whitmont in chapter five, is an archetypal fact. Even the twisted viciousness of E.K. proved to be an infernal attempt at a kind of salvation. To assume, as many have, that religion is merely something which one "believes in," means paying a heavy price for beliefs which leave the sexual sphere unmythologized, unimagined and completely secularized. The experience of being in the grip of an archetype is something to which mere beliefs can hold no candle. The shape and manifestation of the religious instinct is scarcely dependent upon the religious instruction of the Church, which in many cases provides the most meager vessel in which the instinct may be realized and contained. What of the sense of indefinable awe which a child may experience at the opening of a chrysalid, or in turning over a dead rabbit infested with maggots? What of an erotic longing so global that a human beloved is unimaginable, and what of a hatred or sense of expanding power wholly incommensurate with the frail object? Sexuality may also be lived with an appreciation of its symbolic aspect, its relation to the numinous. For some this recognition may be a dire necessity should a neurosis force the matter upon them.

In dealing privately and therapeutically with man *as he is,* traditional moralistic assumptions need be held in abeyance. Unless the analysand be truly psychopathic, he will have moral impulses of his own however walled-in they may be. The analyst must be prepared to accept the numinous in whatever form it may initially appear, though dealing with rape may tax one's will to stay with the old alchemical tenet that "the treasure is found in filth."

The intermingling of religious ideation and sexual psychopathy is in fact not at all uncommon. Krafft-Ebing, for example, records the case of a young man incarcerated for rape-murder. The subject recounted that the thought gradually came to him how pleasurable it would be to stab a pretty young girl in the genitals and behold the blood on his knife. And yet:

> Among his effects were found copies of the objects of phallic cult and obscene pictures painted by himself of Mary's conception and of the "thought of God injected" into the lap of the Virgin.[162]

Groth and Birnbaum cite one case in which a man in his twenties committed a bizarre series of five or more rape-murders in one summer:

> As described in the pathologist's report, each victim had been dismembered into five parts. The skin was peeled off the breasts and vagina. On the legs and buttocks, there were multiple stab wounds and punctures. Stab wounds were also present in the anterior chest wall. Sperm was found in both the vagina and the rectum of the body, and findings were consistent with its having been deposited postmortem.[163]

This sadistic offender, inflated by feelings of omnipotence, was interested in religious matters. Originally of Catholic background, he gave this up at twelve years of age, "but continued to believe in Christ the man."

> After his twelfth birthday, he learned stone masonry and carpentry and described some of the buildings as monuments that his children might look up to. When he was twenty-three years old, he began to accumulate a group of teenage drug users around him, and was called by them "Sire" and "Lord Eric." He called his followers disciples.[164]

This case is reminiscent of Charles Manson's inflated and demonic-messianic pretensions. Here the ritualistic dismemberment, skinning and necrophilia pass beyond considerations of mere sexuality and power to a positively mythological form of acting-out. One thinks again of Hades, Seth or the Tantric Yama, ithyphallic demon of death whose bull descends climaxing upon a corpse. Groth and Birnbaum describe sadistic rapists as typically preoccupied with "the morbid, the occult, the violent and the bizarre,"[165] and characterize the type in two further passages:

> This offender finds the intentional maltreatment of his victim intensely gratifying and takes pleasure in her torment, anguish, distress, helplessness and suffering. The assault usually involves bondage and torture and frequently has a bizarre or ritualistic quality to it. The offender may subject his victim to curious actions, such as clipping her hair, washing or cleansing her body, or forcing her to dress in some specific fashion or behave in some specific way.[166]
>
> He is interested in sadomasochistic pornography and may have a collection of souvenirs or mementoes of his victims, such as photographs and articles of clothing.[167]

The specific choice of victims and the treatment of them, the mementoes, etc., may all possess a specific symbolic value in the psychology of the rapist, though amidst such emotional turmoil— with the perpetrator so completely in the grip of the unconscious— these particulars appear to be less personally than archetypally determined. The history of folk custom and myth abound with instructive parallels. As has been stated, an act of sexual assault or the destruction of a chosen victim is profoundly a matter of the protection of the soul. The routine shaving of all hair from the bodies of so-called witches in the late Middle Ages is only one simple example.

Another insight into the relation of rape and the religious instinct derives from the life of a modern saint, Maria Goretti (1890-1902), and her murderer Allesandro Serenelli. Their story is presented by Brownmiller, who prefaces it with the observation:

Elevated to sainthood for the manner of their violent deaths as much
for the purity of their short lives, Agnes, Agatha, Lucia, Philomena,
Susanna and many others became celebrated in Catholic traditions as
the virgin martyrs. . . . Saint Agnes, the most famous virgin martyr of
them all, was a child of twelve. She was thrown naked into a brothel
as part of the routine punishment of "outrage," but through miraculous intervention her honor was preserved. Virginity intact, little
Agnes was beheaded.[168]

Not atypically, the virginity of the girl is more highly valued by the
Church than her head—even in an instance of divine intervention.
The 13-year-old peasant girl Maria Goretti was likewise lauded for
resisting rape by her half-brother Serenelli. "She used all her efforts
to preserve her chastity," whereupon she died with fourteen stab
wounds in her body. "Six years into his jail sentence, the unremorse-
ful murderer saw a vision of Maria in his cell (she came to him
dressed in white, carrying flowers), and became penitent."[169]

Serenelli, eventually released from prison, visited the mother of
Maria, spent the next 27 years of his life as a Cappucin brother, and
was even present in St. Peter's when his victim was proclaimed
blessed by Pope Pius XII in 1947. The murderer's guilt was apparently washed away and Maria herself was held up, predictably
enough, as a model of the chaste Catholic woman. Nothing of
substance regarding actual attitudes toward women was effected. But
what is important in the present context is the phenomenological
"spectrum" represented by Maria Goretti and her ghostly image
"dressed in white" as external personifications of the anima—the
contrasexual aspect of the masculine psyche—whose role in rape we
shall now examine in more detail.

The Role of the Anima

Anima is the first crucial factor in rape. Without a fundamental
recognition of this archetype, rape as a problem *within* men will
never be grasped. As has already become quite clear, the male
fantasy of woman is the primary factor. As the bearer of the anima
in projection, woman appears as the highest and the lowest which
man stands existentially over against:

Appearing as the Other, woman appears at the same time as an
abundant being in contrast to that existential nothingness of which
man senses in himself; the Other, being regarded as the object in the
eyes of the subject, is regarded *en soi;* therefore as being. In woman is
incarnated in positive form the lack that the existant carries in his
heart, and it is in seeking to be made whole through her that man
hopes to attain self-realization.[170]

Man seeks in woman the Other as Nature and as his fellow being. But we know the ambivalent feelings Nature inspires in man: He exploits her, but she crushes him, he is born of her and dies in her; she is the source of his being, and the realm he subjugates to his will; Nature is a vein of gross material in which the soul is imprisoned, and she is the supreme reality; she is contingence and Idea, the finite and the whole; she is what opposes the Spirit, and the Spirit itself. Now ally, now enemy, she appears as the dark chaos from whence life wells up, as this life itself, and the over-yonder toward which life tends. Woman sums up Nature as Mother, Wife and Idea; these forms mingle and now conflict, and each of them wears a double visage.[171]

Thus the rich and paradoxical characterization of woman as anima by a woman herself of extraordinary insight, Simone de Beauvoir.

Man sees in woman a compelling significance deeply conditioned not only by his personal experience of women, but by a priori psychological factors as well. Jung early described a man's anima, or "feminine soul complex," as deriving from the experience of actual women (beginning with the mother), from his own femininity and from "an inherited collective image of woman ... with the help of which he apprehends the nature of woman."[172] As we know, however, the anima may at times be the source of blatant misapprehensions of women as well, for "so long as the anima is unconscious she is always projected."[173] What the passage from de Beauvoir describes very nicely, Jung makes psychologically explicit: "The anima personifies the total unconscious so long as she is not differentiated as a figure from the other archetypes."[174]

A condition in which the anima is consciously unrealized, and thus left submerged in or contaminated with the whole of the unconscious, constitutes the foundation of all misogynous attitudes. Precisely this blindness sustains as well the collective prejudice which considers woman as the responsible party in sexual assault. One contribution to this state of affairs is the lack of religious representations of the Great Goddess in our Christian tradition. Banished into the unconscious though She be, dreams still lead one to her, with one visage or another. As Jung remarks following a series of dreams in "The Psychological Aspects of the Kore":

From this series and others like it we get an average picture of that strange factor which has such an important part to play in the masculine psyche, and which naïve presumption invariably identifies with certain women, imputing to them all the illusions that swarm in the male Eros.[175]

In rape, "naive" though such presumptions may be, a certain woman becomes the image of a man's ambivalence and the victim of his fear. "It is not that I dread her," one of Karen Horney's patients insisted, "it is that she is malignant, capable of any crime, a beast of prey, a vampire, a witch, insatiable in her desires. She is the very personification of what is sinister."[176] The archetypal depths of this dread have already been examined.

Demanding further consideration and differentiation is the contrast between mother and anima. Much is written of the coldness, seductiveness and ambivalence of rapists' mothers, as if by the term "mother" the most obvious and concrete of facts were being discussed. The very fact that a supposedly scientific theory such as psychoanalysis propounded such a concretistic and reductionistic conception of mother and psychic phenomena in general is itself an indication of the influence of the Great Mother, for she is the reductive archetype par excellence. Despite the Freudian contribution toward seeing sexuality as significant beyond reproduction, as a component of the full range of psychic phenomena, the psyche in that system remains finally reducible to biology and hence to matter. This is nothing less than the feminine in its "lowest" and most concrete manifestation. One spontaneously thinks of the dull concretism of Nicodemus pondering the mystery of rebirth, for the feminine is also spirit. Already reviewed, in chapter four, are the results of that 1954 Rorschach study with its poor male subjects, its condemnation of the evil mothers and wives and its positively stoney concretism.

The significance of the personal mother in early childhood, however important, is later superseded by that of the anima archetype, whose first personification is nonetheless the actual mother. But if the personal mother or contact with her is insufficient, the archetype carries the potential in and of itself to "fill the gap." Recall Jung's view, quoted in chapter five: "It must be remembered that 'mother' is really an imago, a psychic image only." She is also the gateway into the unconscious, the place of origins, as the dream referred to in chapter three of the paradise garden, the fetuses, the model heart and the chirping and crying in the receding darkness nicely reflects. Such a dream constitutes a rather pure glimpse "back through" the mother—the glimpse of quite a reflective young man far along in his analysis. But for many, certainly for the rapist, an initial encounter with the unconscious amounts to a frightening, even unendurable and frantically avoided confrontation with this chaotic urge to life, for the rapist is a veritable automata of just this instinctual force.

In the concrete life situation of a rapist, the dynamics imaged in the above "paradise" dream look very different. Consider the case of a down-and-out young man, severely depressed, working for his father part-time, collecting welfare and living in the basement of his sister's home. He recounted:

I dreaded living there, and I had the feeling they didn't really want me, but I couldn't seem to find myself. I'd get very depressed sometimes and just feel like giving up. I'd get these crying jags. I'd go down into the cellar, and it would be so cold there at night. I was living this kind of life, and I didn't want to. I just didn't care what happened to me. I didn't care about living, but didn't want to die either. I just wanted to take time out for a while and get myself together. I got so depressed. Much of the time I'd cry. I'd go down the cellar in my sister's place and just break up and bawl my eyes out. Then I'd get a grip on myself and I'd go about living my dull life again.[177]

Thus a picture of unreflected regression, a private and pathetic picture most certainly, but—as this particular young man was institutionalized after three court convictions for armed assault and rape— a dangerous one as well. Floundering within the family constellation, this young man is in the grip of the unconscious with no containment of his emotional life; emotionally he is still a child. For such individuals women tend to be less persons than nameless, faceless nonentities swept under with him.

In "The Psychological Aspects of the Kore," Jung states that "in the products of unconscious activity, the anima appears equally as maiden and mother," and cautions against personalistic interpretations.[178] He considers the practical problem of the Demeter/Kore (Persephone) mythologem primarily in regard to feminine psychology, as does Patricia Berry. Citing a series of dreams which include a dying dancer and the crucifixion of a girl, he makes some important observations:

Just as in the preceding cases the sacrifice of a child or a sheep played a part, so here the sacrifice of the maiden hanging on the "cross." The death of the dancer is also to be understood in this sense, for these maidens are always doomed to die, because their exclusive domination of the feminine psyche hinders the individuation process. . . . The "maiden" corresponds to the anima of the man and makes use of it to gain her natural ends, in which illusion plays the greatest role imaginable. But as long as a woman is content to be a *femme à homme*, she has no feminine individuality. She is empty and merely glitters—a welcome vessel for masculine projections.[179]

A transposition of this material into masculine psychology provides an insight into the character of the rapist's anima. Already observed is the maternal anima and its powerful undertow. The "maiden" is a relative nonentity, an insubstantial nymph or siren, allusive and alluring. The anima of the rapist is correspondingly "no feminine individuality" but is unrealized and undifferentiated. Accordingly women are colored by projections and become the hapless victims of a devilish raping Eros. As in the concrete actions of the sexual offender, some of the maidens are indeed doomed to die. The domination of the emotional and imaginal life by such empty, glittering anima figures is an influence of the Great Mother, whose natural ends are antithetical to the individuation of the single personality.

One may recall the intentionality of the goddess Gaia, described earlier by Patricia Berry. To what end are these maidens pursued, raped or destroyed? By whom or what? An exploration of these most central questions may best be pursued through a young man's dream in which the fate of a young woman is a central issue:

> I talk with a morally indignant uncle. I have come home from college and accidentally run over six local men with the car. I injure all, kill one. Beneath the earth with him there is a small metal bow and arrow.
>
> I then visit friends my age who are all more established professionally. Older men also.
>
> Then in a boat offshore by the ocean are many men—all Jews—like Odysseus and his sailors. They drag a net to catch fish. I would like to do this too.
>
> Then: Either at a party, or at the home of Mick [childhood friend] or in a restaurant. A party is being planned. I notice a woman there—she has luscious voluptuous breasts and a low-necked dress on, sort of an 18th-century style. I would love to rape her with a vengeance—to really take her. But I am sort of on my way to school, the way I went when I was a kid and I'm somehow improper.
>
> In a room where a party is to be held. An analyst is there and also his wife. So is Dr. Benjamin Spock. I am impressed at what notable friends Mick has at the party. A guest poet is also there. The central entertainment will be his reading. Then all kinds of weird people begin to arrive and I grow uncomfortable—sort of improper again. No one seems to relate to one another too well. The poet ponders a while, but then to the approval of all announces that he will recite *The One Hundred and Twenty Days....* "In Sodom?" I interrupt. "Marquis de Sade?" He replies, "All of it!" It is the analyst who requests especially the reciting of a passage called "The Torture of Rose Marie."
>
> Not wanting to be there at all, I get up and start walking quickly down the street to my apartment, but with no real understanding of why I have left. I think I might go back later, but then another fellow —a veritable alter ego—is walking down the street too and he is GOING MAD! He bears a curse for having left the party, somehow.
>
> This crazy alter ego goes rushing back to his single apartment and begins desperately drawing pictures and hanging them around the room, as if he would go totally insane if he didn't draw the pictures. But the mood gets the better of him, and seeing visions, he begins jerking all around the room—battered one way and the other by unseen forces. At one point a hand comes out from a niche in the wall and shoves a marijuana cigarette in his mouth which he starts smok-

ing. Then out in front of the apartment he sees a strange Negro man
with a large black and white dog on a leash casually out for a walk.
This causes a deep shudder and terror in the alter ego and he is going
insane at the end of the dream.

This dreamer was not a rapist, although rape had been a recurrent fantasy. He recalled, for instance, ending a relationship with a
girlfriend at age 15 with a self-pitying note to her signed "Richard
Speck" (a famous American mass-murderer), as well as an occasion
when he and an adolescent boyfriend had excitedly read aloud a
pornographic story entitled "The Night of the Rapist." He even
recalled a dream the same boyfriend had spontaneously related, of a
huge underground prison in which he kept hundreds of women in
chains, ruling over them and sexually abusing them at his will. The
young man's first experience of orgasm had taken place at the age of
13 during homosexual experimentation with this friend. Fatefully
enough, seven years later the friend married a young woman—
pregnant by him—whom the analysand had earlier pointed out as a
sexually very willing young lady.

In the analysis the young man was most specifically concerned
with finding a means to ground his problematic overexcitability, and
come to terms with a rather hysterical feminine side of himself
which he clearly intuited. Having had a highly stressed relationship
with his father, he was at times obsessed with questions about his
"maturity." His mother was a simple woman, loving and living for
her children.

The morally indignant uncle in the dream is a real person—a
stern superego figure—with whom, though admiring him, the dreamer felt no more comfortable that he would with the local working
men. The unconscious destruction of one of these men reminded the
dreamer of an incident in which a local man protected him while he
was being harassed by outsiders. Yet in the dream these are injured,
and one is killed. "Bow and arrow" were associated with Indian
initiation and with Eros. Bow and arrow and the dead protector/
workman suggest an unconscious Eros function, a lack of relationship between disparate aspects of the analysand's masculinity. This
lack of relatedness characterized the mood of the party as well. The
wistful visiting of established professional men reflects the same
problem—that of "maturity." The Jews as "sailors of Odysseus"
coalesce as an image of men banded together in a shared esprit de
corps, providing food and seeking spirit (fish)—but the dreamer only
looks on.

Considered as masculine elements of the psyche fraternally
bound, the fishermen have a sense of futurity, but the dream takes a
retrogressive gradient as if to go back and link up with something in

the past. An anima atmosphere characteristically has an historical quality. With great consistency men seek to reassure themselves of their masculinity vis-à-vis women to the degree they doubt it in relation to other men. Our dreamer watches the men go by, then finds himself a mere adolescent, back at the home of a childhood friend, and ready to rape "with a vengeance" the woman with the "luscious voluptuous breasts." That this may be taking place in a restaurant, and given the marijuana cigarette later in the dream, we may see the oral instinct, the longing for unconsciousness and hence the mother as most evident. The dreamer recognized the 18th-century garb of the woman as corresponding to that of female character types appearing in the work of de Sade, with which he was familiar. Indeed he had long been intrigued and distressed at the fascination which books such as *The One Hundred and Twenty Days of Sodom* had for him.

The analyst of the dream and his wife and the famous American pediatrician, Benjamin Spock, were all persons whom the analysand considered far more learned and mature than himself; though concerning the former two he had felt considerable suspicion regarding their "morality." The presence of Dr. Spock suggests that some treatment for a very youthful aspect of the dreamer's personality might be in the making. Furthermore, an association to Spock consisted of recalling an inspiring lecture by him which touched the dreamer seven years earlier—a time of tremendous psychic disorientation. Particularly distressing in the dream was finding three respected persons at a party centering around "The Torture of Rose Marie"—which is obviously an anxiety-provoking theme.

Most puzzling of all is the "curse" which lay on the dissociated alter ego—the kindred figure whose further dissociation the dream ego witnessed. This figure brought up further recollections of the same traumatic period seven years before, the dreamer then a university student with a number of years of marked heterosexual promiscuity and drug usage behind him. It was also a time of complete financial dependence on his father. The dreamer recalled making drawings at the time in a manner similar to the frantic efforts of the alter ego. Clearly this figure is a resurfacing image of his old behavior, presently functioning as an element of the personal shadow.

Cursed as the alter ego is for his untimely departure, it can be assumed that some very specific reason lay in the presence of both him, and by association the dreamer himself, at the party with its ever stranger gathering of people. As both mature known persons and "all kinds of weird people" begin gathering, so likewise the battering "unseen forces" threaten the figure who has fled into his narcotized solitude. But the curse he bears presses upon both the dream ego and his psychotic compatriot a need to confront the mystery of the party, as well as the necessity of imaging what forces are at work in the most literal way—in pictures.

Fortunate for present purposes is that the young man brought a drawing from seven years earlier (opposite). He also went on from the dream experience to spontaneously write an enlightening active imagination. The single room, the compulsive drawing and the use of marijuana reflect the former student days and the maternal vessel in which the then young narcissist had remained enfolded. The autonomous hand coming from the niche in the wall only enforces the view that the mother (the autonomous hand a virtual umbilical cord) is playing her hand in the crippled situation. (A later dream, presented above in chapter three, with niche, crying child and chirping bird, shows quite a transformed vision of the same maternal background.)

A particularly puzzling element of the present dream was that such terror should be evoked by the appearance of a rather relaxed, gentle, Negro man. Hardly a raging hound of hell, though one thinks of Cerberus in this context, the dog is black and white and calmly under the control of his easy-going master. The dog's coloration suggests some possibility of integrating conscious and unconscious. One might hastily term the black man a "shadow figure" and leave it at that, but the term allows finer differentiation. In discussing black persons in dreams, Hillman points out that "the Black Man is also Thanatos." He further suggests that one may

> consider black persons in dreams in terms of their resemblance with this underworld context. Their concealing and raping attributes belong to the "violating" phenomenology of Hades, . . . just as their pursuit resembles the hounding by the death demons. They are returning ghosts from the repressed netherworld—not merely from the repressed ghetto. Their message is psychic before it is vital. They bring one down and steal one's "goods" and menace the ego behind its locked doors.[180]

From the black man of the dream one receives more the impression of a transforming agent, a future equilibrium, but also of death to the rigid and restricted orientation of the alter ego. In light of the black man's underworldly connotation and his calm control of the "animal of the threshold," the dead workingman with the bow and arrow, as well as the desire to draw fish from the ocean may be recalled. The death of the old *participation mystique* (the strong unconscious bond with the mother) carries the possibility of integrating the kindred masculine elements within the personality of the

Young man's drawing of anal penetration by a cross.

dreamer—an initiation through symbolic death into the "men's hut" in which Eros plays a crucial role.

The inner analyst and his wife, the pediatrician Spock and the poet all favoring the idea of torture raises obvious difficulties for the concrete and moralizing diurnal mind, and rightly so. Were the dream to evoke no moral conflict we would have a sorry case indeed. The first portion of the present study dealt extensively enough with the grounds for such apprehension. At this juncture however a strictly symbolic perspective has been adopted. In the present case, the dreamer proceeded in this way to produce a lengthy and vivid active imagination which he titled, "The One-Hundred-and-Twenty-First Day: The Dispatch of the Lovely Rose Marie." In true Sadean style it lingers on details of the furnishings of a chamber of debauchery and the sexual-sadistic murder of the young woman. At its outset the girl had been found hiding in a chapel, "dozing before the thoroughly amusing Botticelli Madonna and Child that hangs above the altar there."

The analysand's text continued:

> The poor child was apparently unaware not only that the former tenants had long been done away with, and likewise most all the vestiges of their quaint little faith, but that the madonna was left behind precisely to grace our own dark "chapel" on this final day of our immersion in ecstasy. Benjamin [Spock] had gone to secure it, and found our missing one there before the canvas—the last reflection of her naive hopes.

The male participants induce the young woman to dance, rape her polymorphously and then, releasing numerous poisonous snakes around her, wait to observe her end. All the while the wife of the analyst (Paulette) has played on a harpsichord. The analysand's fantasy concluded with the snakes poisoning him as well, after he had shot the other men. He was surprised at the way the fantasy ended:

> Rose Marie had risen in the last frantic throws of her poisoning and cried out in a long and eerie wail. She crept breathlessly toward me, her eyes filled with deep and sinking terror, but then—to my amazement—she began to *laugh*, a high uncanny laughter that became one with the sound of the harpsichord. I saw through darkening eyes that Paulette had however vanished, but the merry current of the music, formerly so rhapsodic, rushed on and on, indistinguishable from the pitched and continuing cry of the now expired Marie.

In the dream leading to this active imagination the dreamer's alter ego was the object of a profound threat—and from the drawing of seven years earlier one can see that he himself was being psychically raped by violating contents of the unconscious. Interesting is the fact that the face in the lower left of the picture represents a "naive little Catholic girl with her rosary," opposite a death's head, with a less distinguished hairy-eyed face in between. The homosexual aspect and the anal penetration will be further considered below. Suffice it for the present to identify the alter ego of the dream with the violated figure in the seven-year-old drawing, and in turn with the psychological state of the dreamer at that time—characterized by identification with a naive and undifferentiated anima, a floundering insecure masculinity as well as a strong *participation* with the mother. Of central concern now however is the rape of the woman and the phenomenology of the anima.

In addition to the maternal background represented by the single apartment and the "drug-pushing" hand, a number of anima images appear, including the woman in 18th-century dress, the young Rose Marie and finally the harpsichordist and analyst's wife, Paulette. Especially in the active imagination Rose Marie comes into her own as one of those maidens "always doomed to die," because—to echo Jung—her exclusive domination of the feminine aspect of the dreamer's personality hinders the individuation process. Considering the fearful inability of both the dream ego and the alter ego to face up to the necessity of her fate, and the psychotic demise of the second figure, this hindrance is manifest. The dreamer's own raping and murderous shadow, the emptiness and inadequacy of the anima image, his former impoverished emotional life and lack of relatedness—all remain most problematic.

Accepting this dream and proceeding with its explicit demands for transformation resulted in a relatively conscious experience of the instinct and an enactment, however impure, of that central archetype of the individuation process, *sacrifice.* This introduces the final perspective of the present study on the dynamics and psychological meaning of rape: that *the impulse to rape carries within it the impulse to sacrifice resulting in a transformation of that same instinct.* A number of intermediary considerations remain, however, before an elaboration of this central theme, in the final chapter.

After shooting all the other men, the analysand holds in his hands a snake whose poison begins to overtake him as the fantasy concludes. Furthermore, he displayed a positively boyish amusement at his "literary" production. It must be borne in mind that this is but one glimpse into a long analytical process. Instructive for the present discussion of the anima is the fact that though Rose Marie's carnal remains lay devastated, the fantasy apparently continues past even its written conclusion in the pitched cry and the harpsichord music. The musician too had vanished. Whatever "essence" Rose Marie secretly shared with Paulette proves to be quite indestructible—even given the erotic violence and the venomous execution. Jung has pointed out that with the anima "illusion plays the greatest role imaginable," which is certainly the case here. Whatever "she" may ultimately be, her completely nonrational, illusive and highly autonomous nature makes a vivid impression. Jung often describes the anima as the "archetype of life" and emphasizes that:

It is a "factor" [*facere:* "to make"] in the proper sense of the word. Man cannot make it; on the contrary, it is always the *a priori* element in his moods, reactions, impulses, and whatever else is spontaneous in psychic life. It is something that lives of itself, that makes us live; it is a life behind consciousness that cannot be completely integrated with it, but from which, on the contrary, consciousness arises.[181]

Her autonomous and "divine" nature make the anima a psychic figure to achieve a relationship with, not simply to identify with or futilely attempt to destroy. Here the analysand displays both latter alternatives, each with their attendant problems, reflected rather clearly in the old drawing. The mysterious conclusion of the active imagination displays the autonomy of the anima. She is the greatest of storytellers—the actress, the theater, the cinema, the zoo—she who is "thronged round with images of all creation." The rapist is her prisoner, willy-nilly, in hate and desire. He assaults his victim, but "she" whirls on about her affairs, her guise partially dependent on the reflecting eye of the ego, but finally inscrutable.

A striking example of the anima appears in de Sade's *One Hundred and Twenty Days of Sodom* itself, that wearying yarn of lust-murder which grinds on through nearly 500 pages. A striking document of instinct and imagination, this work fantasizes the digestive heat of a psychoid realm. Presiding over the carnage and spinning the images of the instinct are three imposing and experienced whores:

> The three storytellers, magnificently dressed as upper class Parisian courtesans, were seated below the throne upon a couch, and Madame Duclos, the month's narrator, in very scant and elegant attire, rouged and heavily bejewelled, having taken her place on the stage thus began the story of what had occurred in her life, into which account she was, with all pertinent details, to insert the first one hundred and fifty passions designated by the title of *simple passions.*[182]

A corresponding example of the anima appears in the *1001 Nights* in which, amongst the multitude of bedmates beheaded and disposed of by King Shahrian, Scheherazade alone prolongs her life by telling a grand series of stories.

Both these examples, and Charles Manson's statement, "The world we live in is a woman's thought," as well as the above dream material, show the anima as an autonomous urge to life, instinctual yet imagistic, and intimately associated with sexual violence, particularly when she is left unconscious and undifferentiated. Ultimately de Sade reflects not merely human sexuality or power, but the stark dynamism of life and death which we all carry deep within us—a timeless primary process of the organic world.

The Reflecting Vessel of Eros

Fantasy such as de Sade's seems to signal a return to the instinctual mother, to the physical facts, and indeed his concretism takes us no farther. But psychologically this is a confrontation with the affective *imago,* with the final background remaining unknown. However compelling a dream, a fantasy, or even the scientist's "empirical data" may be in leading one to believe he is observing "instinctual processes," one sees rather an image, which points immediately to the action of spirit. The realization results from a third, inner eye turned to the anima. Gradually she sloughs off her purely instinctual significance and may be recognized as a preeminent faculty of *imagination.* The process constitutes an initiatory step—the true constellation of the anima as spirit in contrast to the instinctual mother. Jung has often stressed the extreme difficulty and disruptive possibilities of facing the psychic background, stating, for example:

> The relation with the anima is again a test of courage, an ordeal by fire for the spiritual and moral forces of man. We should never forget that in dealing with the anima we are dealing with psychic facts which have never been in man's possession before, since they were always found "outside" his psychic territory, so to speak, in the form of projections.[183]

Working analytically with rape fantasies means observing this persistent and lengthy battle, filled with illusion and backward steps. But a gradual facing-off does take place. Especially when the analysand is young or still immersed in the mother-world, possessing no real capacity for grasping the anima, is she problematic in the manner Jung describes. A heroic struggle for the liberation of the ego from the unconscious indeed constitutes the central work. As the representative of the whole of the unconscious—the womb of all nascent masculine and feminine elements of the personality—the maternal anima carries Eros within her and presides over the Eros principle. With the progressive differentiation of the anima, however, and the constellation of the personal anima or *soror mystica,* the man who pursues her with Eros comes into his own masculinity —however active an exponent of the feminine and of relationship he may be.

Jung identifies the Eros principle with the feminine, but a perspective which would consider Eros as a masculine figure in his own right has contrastingly been elaborated by James Hillman and others.[184] In his article "Anima," Hillman discusses these subtleties.

> Even where Jung speaks of "four stages of eroticism" (*CW* 16, par. 361) and correlates the four stages of erotic phenomenology with four

grades of the anima (Eve, Helen, Mary, Sophia), the feminine images are not the eros itself but the objects of its longing (*pothos*). A drive has a corresponding projection, a goal it seeks, a grail to hold its blood. These containers may be represented by the anima images which Jung describes, and a quality of eros may be correlated with each of these figures, but the figures are not the eros. . . . but the beloveds; they are reflections of love. They are the means by which eros can see itself. . . . The images are soul-portraits by means of which eros is drawn into the psychic field and can be witnessed as a psychic event.[185]

Distinguishing Eros from the object of its pursuit is particularly important in application to the problem of rape. Jung speaks of the problems arising from the projected anima image, and indeed, we have already reviewed the worst results of this. But our earlier shifting of consideration from the archetype of the the Great Mother to the "Terrible Male" within her pertains here as well; and again this shift is made not as a gesture to feminism but in recognition of an archetypal factor crucial to the problem of rape. However intra-psychic our focus has become, the anima, as Hillman points out, is the reflecting object of longing and not the pursuing Eros itself. To view her receding allure one-sidedly would be to maintain more than a trace of the misogynous tendency previously discussed. De-spite a deeper penetration we would be playing Krafft-Ebing's old game.

A practical example of this problem may be taken from the autobiography of the well-known American rapist and revolutionary Black Panther, Eldridge Cleaver. The following passage from *Soul On Ice*, written in a California prison by this extremly passionate black man, vividly records a battle with one image whose power would not abate:

I became an extreme iconoclast. Any affirmation made by anyone around me became a target for tirades of criticism.

This little game got good to me and I got good at it. I attacked all forms of piety, loyalty and sentiment: marriage, love, God, patriotism, the Constitution, the founding fathers, law, concepts of right-wrong-good-evil, all forms of ritualized and conventional behavior. As I pranced about, club in hand, seeking new idols to smash, I encoun-tered really for the first time in my life, with any seriousness, the Ogre, rising up before me in the mist. I discovered, with alarm, that the Ogre possessed a tremendous and dreadful power over me, and I didn't understand this power or why I was at its mercy. I tried to repudiate the Ogre, root it out of my heart as I had done God, Constitution, principles, morals, and values—but the Ogre had its claws buried in the core of my being and refused to let go. I fought frantically to be free, but the Ogre only mocked me and sank its claws deeper into my soul. I knew then I had found an important key, that if I conquered the Ogre and broke its power over me I would be free. But I also knew that it was a race against time and that if I did not win I would certainly be broken and destroyed. I, a black man, confronted the Ogre—the white woman.[186]

This torturous initial insight came *before* Cleaver began his career as a rapist. He left prison with, as he says, "an antagonistic, ruthless attitude toward white women" and overflowing with feelings which could be summed up in the lines of a poem he wrote entitled "To a White Girl":

> I love you
> Because you're white,
> Not because you're charming
> Or bright.
> Your whiteness
> Is a silky thread
> Snaking through my thoughts
> In redhot patterns
> Of lust and desire.
>
> I hate you
> Because you're white
> Your white meat
> Is nightmare food.
> White is
> The Skin of Evil.
> You're my Moby Dick,
> White witch,
> Symbol of the rope and hanging tree,
> Of the burning cross.
>
> Loving you thus
> And hating you so,
> My heart is torn in two,
> Crucified.[187]

Cleaver speaks for himself of the anima who drew him toward crucifixion, but he reacted by choosing other victims. The manner in which he responds to the "White Girl" represents one more instance of the classic male error of seeing the outer woman as the ogre. His attitude carried over into practice:

> Rape was an insurrectionary act. It delighted me that I was defying and trampling upon the white man's law, upon his system of values, and that I was defiling his women—and this point, I believe was the most satisfying to me because I was resentful over the historical fact of how the white man had used the black woman.[188]

Yet, Cleaver states that he "started out by practicing on black girls in the ghetto."[189] Hardly acting in a revolutionary fashion, he simply falls into the historical pattern of viewing women as masculine property. His crime is only secondarily against the white man; most centrally it is a crime against women, black and white.

Assuming that the anima is the reflecting image of Eros, the question must be asked just what ogre is reflected in the image of the white girl rising up "in the mist" of Cleaver's imagination. "The Ogre only mocked me and sank its claws deeper into my soul," says Cleaver, and though he uses the term "soul" quite generally, I understand and read it as some iconoclastic, attacking, impious and dreadfully powerful force that sent Cleaver forth from prison on a raping spree. His victims were *not* the "Ogre," but rather the nameless, faceless women who served as little more than the empty and glittering vessels of his own masculine projections. The anima image *reflects* the ogre. But before pursuing the real ogre, let the anima herself be further considered.

Eldridge Cleaver's story did not end at this point; his Eros found quite another reflecting vessel on a clear Mediterranean evening ten years later after years of exile in Algeria and France. Agitated, contemplating suicide and gazing out to sea from his balcony, Cleaver watched the play of shadows across the moon. As one interviewer relates:

> He suddenly saw his own image take shape. He recognized it instantly —the same profile he had seen a million times on the Black Panther posters.... He tried to control a growing apprehension by telling himself he was just tripping out on the moon, but it was impossible to reassure himself. The feeling of dread expanded, intensified; and overwhelming fear was welling up inside him, like death. That was it —he felt in contact with death itself. He wondered if seeing oneself in the moon was some kind of premonition and wished he knew something about folklore. He began to tremble as the inner fright mounted, and then the trembling got worse, coming from somewhere deep inside, shaking his soul.... Then his image rolled away, but in its place came a succession of familiar faces—Fidel Castro, Karl Marx, Friedrich Engles, Mao Tse-tung, all his old heroes. What was happening to him anyway? Was he finally losing his mind as he had lost his life's momentum and purpose? Then, of all faces in heaven and earth, the face of Jesus Christ formed out of the moon shadows.[190]

This experience with its emotional aftershocks constituted the decisive rebirth experience of Eldridge Cleaver, who at present is an evangelical Christian. Whatever the future holds for him, regardless of how simple an enantiodromia may have taken place, and however he may currently imagine the "Ogre," his case, like that of Allesandro Serenelli, clearly portrays the propensity of the anima toward spirit. She reflects and contains the desire of Eros and serves as the vessel of psychic transformation. These factors are recognized only through the experience of the anima as an inner factor, be it through the individuation process as it is followed and supported in analytical treatment or through the kind of spontaneous soul experience just described.

Cleaver's story recalls the suicide attempt of Siddhartha in the novel of the same name by Hermann Hesse. Wearied and despairing from long immersion in sensual excess, he is about to plunge himself into a river sprinkled with reflecting stars. A voice from within stops him on the brink; he sleeps deeply and awakens to a new life.

An even more striking amplification appears in the itinerant misadventures of Lucius in *The Golden Ass*. The turning point in this Roman tale by Apuleius bespeaks the contrast between the soul imago projected outside and the realization of it as an internal factor. The early narrative finds Lucius transformed into an ass through the abuse of a witch's magic salve, and his continually hampered search for the antidotal rose which leads him into progressively more debasing situations. Finally scheduled to be the star of a pornographic show in an arena before a jeering crowd, this human ass can bear no more. Galloping from the place to the quiet of a seashore by night, the despairing creature falls weeping upon the sand. The Great Goddess then appears to him as Isis with the moon, to instruct and guide him to the healing rose, humanity and on to a renewed spiritual development.

The woman with whom he was to have had sex and the rowdy crowd of the arena may be taken as images of the near complete exteriorization of the soul, while Isis as the spiritual anima brings inner healing and inspires a spiritual development leading Lucius on to the priesthood of Isis and Osiris. The Goddess explains, "My name is One, my appearances manifold . . . ," and does appear as the correlative unity of a host of goddesses. The internalization of psychic life to which the spiritual anima gives birth revolutionizes the personality in the deepest sense. The numinous power of the archetype transforms blind eroticism and prompts a mysterious inner grace. As Isis assures her reborn followers:

"Remember well, however, and keep this thought locked up in your inmost soul, that the course of life which remains to you is pledged to me till the moment of your dying breath. It is no injustice that you should owe your entire life to her whose beneficent action has enabled you to take your place among mankind. But you shall live in blessedness! Under my protection you shall live gloriously! And when you have measured your alloted course and descended to the grave, there too in the hemisphere below, you shall behold me as a light amidst the darkness of Acheron and a queen in the palace of Styx, and you shall dwell yourself in Elysian Fields and win my favor by unceasing adoration."[191]

In the light of rebirth experiences such as Serenelli's, that of Cleaver or Apuleius may be seen not only as the transformed image of the anima, but also of the masculine, as Christ, Osiris, etc. It is no coincidence that the best-known version of the fairytale "Amor and Psyche" comes from *The Golden Ass.* There the tale is told to a young girl in a cave by an old crony who accompanies the band of kidnapping thieves. The transformation of the figure of Psyche from an unconscious, pretty girl into a goddess is simultaneous with the transformation of an unseen and monstrous lover into transcending Eros himself.

Prominent among Jung's examples of the transformative significance of the archetype of the anima is a 3rd-century Christian document, *The Shepherd of Hermas,* in which he traces "a characteristic transition from the worship of women to the worship of the soul."[192] Hermas, a Christian married and with children, came upon a woman (Rhoda) bathing in the Tiber. She aroused his erotic interest, which the text betrays by its amusing and repressive tone: "How happy I would be if I had a wife of such beauty and distinction. This was my only thought, and no other, not one."[193] Through Hermas' allegiance to principles more comprehensive than a merely biological evaluation of women and the corresponding repression of the erotic element, in progressive dreams and visions a compensatory internal image was constellated. Jung comments:

> For if, in face of the overwhelming might of passion, which puts one human being wholly at the mercy of another, the psyche succeeds in building up a counterposition so that, at the height of passion, the boundlessly desired object is unveiled as an idol and man is forced to his knees before the divine image, then the psyche has delivered him from the curse of the object's spell. . . .
>
> This mechanism obviously worked in the case of Hermas. The transformation of Rhoda into a divine mistress deprived the actual object of her provocative and destructive power and brought Hermas under the law of his own soul and its collective determinants.[194]

Jung goes on to amplify the symbolism of the anima as the transformative vessel: Mary as *thalamus* or "bridal chamber," the Egyptian irrigation pot as the vessel of the "fecundation of Isis by Osiris," etc., [195] thus intuiting her lofty spiritual dimension. But he also keeps his commentary down to earth, for instance by referring to occasional incidents in which "natives in the bush kill a woman and take out her uterus for use in magical rites"! The example (taken from Wallis Budge) is Egyptian, but represents a tendency alien to neither Christianity nor the problem of rape, namely the inclination of the masculine out of fear to seek to dominate and appropriate the feminine. The pristine aerial pole of the anima is again but one pole of the archetype, balanced—as has been seen with the masculine—by its chthonic counterpart. Consciousness changes, and with it the counterposition of opposing contents within the unconscious. Hence the constellation of the anima; her guise from above or below will change.

Hermas was a single individual who lived within a specific *Zeit-geist*. His age was full of optimism in the Church. *The Shepherd of Hermas* "is emphatic on the point: he who fears God cannot be affected by the Devil; Satan himself takes flight when he comes up against a strong resistance."[196] The new dispensation of spiritual integrity in which men such as Hermas thrived was embodied in the sheltering figure of Ecclesia, the Roman Catholic Church. But any period of such satisfactory containment and reflection of the religious impulse in the collective body of the Church or in the individual soul image passes the prime of its integrity. So it is that instances of a numinous, transforming experience of the virgin anima—of Grace—may be vital and recurring in the individuation process, but nevertheless leave one still an ordinary man with a shadow in an everyday world.

The Catholic Church, transient in time and grand thesis that it was, carried within its very stringency the seeds of its own doubts—its own "natives in the bush" who, as inquisitors of papal appointment, had by the end of the 15th century burned thousands of heretics and "witches" of whom by far the majority were women. An important component of this was the exclusive reign of the Virgin as the collective image of the spiritual anima. Jung speaks of her background in paganism and Gnosticism, and of the result of her exaggeration in Catholicism:

> Official Christianity, therefore, absorbed certain Gnostic elements that manifested themselves in the worship of woman and found a place for them in an intensified worship of Mary.... The assimilation of these elements to the Christian symbol nipped in the bud the psychic culture of the man; for his soul, previously reflected in the image of the chosen mistress, lost its individual form of expression through this absorption. Consequently, any possibility of an individual differentiation of the soul was lost when it became repressed in the collective worship.[197]

With this process came not only a crippling of the "psychic culture of the man," but worse consequences of Mariolatry—denigration of women, the witchhunts, the burnings.

Virginity as a Masculine Ideal

The equation of women with either virgin or whore continues to the present day, and crops up not infrequently in the comments of the rapist. Burgess and Holmstrom discuss "Sexual Reputation: The Madonna-Whore Complex":

> Individual women are seldom thought of as having integrated person-
> alities that encompass both maternal love and erotic desires. Instead,
> they are categorized into one-dimensional types. They are maternal or
> they are sexy. They are good or they are bad. They are madonnas or
> they are whores.[198]

The split between maternal and erotic qualities has already been shown to be essential to the separation of son and mother—of ego-consciousness and the maternal unconscious—and in light of the mythologem of Demeter and Kore as well as contrasts between the Earth Mother and the *soror mystica* or spiritual anima, this appears to be a deep and widespread archetypal pattern.

An old and closely related problem is that of *virginity as a masculine ideal.* Brownmiller writes of the historical male concern for "damaged goods." What sort of "damage" is incurred by the man whose Kore anima is raped and falls in the sway of the archetypal masculine? Most simply, virginity in psychological terms bespeaks the integrity of the personality, its sense of wholeness and self-possession. Whatever degree of consciousness may be developed, or virtual adaptation of the personality achieved, the anima as the emotional and imaginal vessel of consciousness remains liable to renewed penetration from outside, e.g., the concrete world and the collective unconscious. Owing to the crucial importance of the emotional atmosphere and imaginative contents of ego-consciousness, the nature of this virginity need be further explored.

The following anecdote, reminiscent of the divine dilemma in *The Book of Enoch,* clearly images the intended sovereignty of the Almighty and its corresponding virgin ideal—to say nothing of Yahweh's own backside:

> Christians, seeking data on the fall of angels and the origins of devils,
> received from an Albigensian heretic an account that was to have
> some influence upon later theologians. Satan, the Albigensians re-
> vealed, was attempting to recruit angels to his own ranks and tempted
> them with word pictures of the daughters of men and the ecstacies of
> the sexual embrace. When they failed to respond to his descriptions,
> he made a hole in the wall of heaven and brought a woman and
> placed her just outside the hole. The angels, seeing her, were awak-
> ened to lust and swarmed out through the hole. Finally God, seeing
> what was happening, and perceiving that the entire population of
> heaven might be lost if he failed to act, plugged the gap in his wall,
> locking out all those angels who had already departed. These became
> and remained the followers of Satan.[199]

Here the wall of heaven corresponds symbolically to the Immaculate

Virgin. The casting out of unclean demons is commonplace in legend; for example:

> Saint Thomas saved from the unwelcome attentions of a lustful demon a beautiful woman who came to him for help. The demon had raped her nightly for five years, but Saint Thomas "sealed her" in the name of the Father, the Son and the Holy Ghost, so that the demon could no longer penetrate her.[200]

Not only under Christianity did the inflated ideal of virginity create an absurd double standard:

> Christian virgins, by Roman law, had to be raped before they could be executed—a function frequently performed by the executioner—since it was not permissible in Rome to put a virgin to death. But Basil the Great in his book *On True Virginity* had given assurance that in such cases God "rendered vain the assaults of sinners upon their flesh and kept their bodies unsoiled by the miracle of His divine power."[201]

Such an outpouring of "divine benevolence" has already been seen in the case of St. Agatha. Roman vestal virgins who had broken their vows of chastity were buried alive and Church authorities in the Middle Ages were known to enforce the virgin ideal with the help of masons, who would promptly wall-in the guilty sister.[202]

Plainly to be seen is the manner in which the lofty ideal of virginity has its contour in the "demonic woman," while doing absolutely nothing to curtail the demonic power necessary to destroy a woman not living up to it. "He wishes to possess her: behold him the possessed himself!"[203] Simone de Beauvoir characterizes the woman's dilemma in this historical and psychological current in remarks which at the same time reflect the phenomenology of the anima:

> If she agrees to deny her animality, woman—from the very fact that she is the incarnation of sin—will be also the most radiant incarnation of the triumph of the elect who have conquered sin. . . . The Mother of Christ is framed in glory; she is the inverse aspect of Eve the sinner, she crushes the serpent underfoot; she is the mediatrix of salvation, as Eve was of damnation. . . . *this is the supreme masculine victory*, consummated in the cult of the Virgin—it is the rehabilitation of woman through the accomplishment of her defeat.[204]

The archetypal tendency of the virgin anima to gravitate toward, or be taken by, the sovereign Father above appears also in Egypt and Greece. The Great Goddess Isis "lost her supreme power as goddess mother" while remaining "generous, smiling, kind, and good, the magnificent wife of Osiris."[205] And again Pallas Athene was gradually transformed into an abstract and virginal ideal. Originally both "Athena" and "Pallas" denoted local Kore figures, maidens of the early Athenians and the clan of the *Pallantidae* respectively—daughters of the Great Goddess in pre-Olympic Greece and intimately related to *Ge* and *Chthon,* i.e., the underworld. As Jane Harrison explains:

> The rising of democracy not unnaturally revived the ancient figure of the Kore, but in reviving her they sharply altered her being and reft from her much of her beauty and reality. They made her a sexless thing, neither man nor woman; she is laden with attributes . . . charged with intended significance, but to the end she remains manufactured, unreal and never convinces us.[206]

Harrison speaks of the birth of Pallas Athene from the head of Zeus, and points out how it remained a "desperate theological expedient to rid an earthbound Kore of her matriarchal conditions."[207] Ideal though she may have become as the personification and protector of the *polis* of Athens, one is persuaded to favor Harrison's judgment:

> We cannot love a goddess who on principle forgets the Earth from which she sprang; always from the lips of the Lost Leader we hear the shameful denial: "There is no mother bore me for her child, I praise the man in all things (save for marriage), Wholehearted am I, strongly for the Father!"[208]

Inspired by such a conception of the goddess might well have been the Greek man in the dream with which this book began. The soul image loses its connection with earth, becoming a transient idea. We owe many of our highest ideals to this upward tendency of the spirit, as may be seen in the feminine personifications for the Church, the Synagogue, Helvetia, Liberty, Harmony, Truth and Wisdom. But by Wisdom, one may understand also a sober acceptance of the fact that evils—and rape among them—may persist as much because we are possessed by ideals as for the lack of them.

7

The Homosexual Component

Power and Eros

However great a concern the present study has maintained for the rapist's relationship with women and his own feminine side, our final concern is the development of the man as a man. The homosexual component of his psychology is crucial for this development in that its dynamics function both through the partial feminine identification of its exponents and simultaneously over against the feminine principle which opposes masculine spirit.

The existence of latent homosexual tendencies in the unconscious is by no means characteristic of rapists alone, but is a ubiquitous phenomenon with a decisive characterological and developmental significance. Obvious in what follows is that the man is prepared to shore up his masculinity in the use of sexual force with his fellows as well as with women. More essential is the fact that the individuating principle expresses its own intentionality in all of the various relations of Eros to its objects, as an attacking "Ogre" or in its highest refinement.

Homosexuality is one oft-mentioned component in the psychology of men who rape women. Insight into this problem may be obtained through an examination of homosexual rape, whether actual or in dreams, a subject which has recently received increasing attention. Many men, insensitive to a problem so apparently remote from their outer lives, might at least have their attention compelled by an inner experience of rape such as this one recorded by a male dreamer who encounters a suspicious pair of men:

> . . . after talking with these guys, they say I had best leave since even though they are lovers, they could without the least pang or hesitation slice me up and murder me with their knives. I run then—run away, though I see horrifying scenes in a hallway and am further threatened with being stabbed to death in the dark. . . . It is then suddenly the middle of a hot, sweaty night in Hollywood and I have just been raped by a strong, whiskered and repulsive man. I struggle to keep from remembering the scene.

A recent issue of the *American Journal of Psychiatry* includes a report by Nicholas Groth on males who had assaulted other males.[209] Groth points out that in the consenting sexual relations one-half of these offenders were heterosexual, some bisexual and a

101

minority exclusively homosexual. In half the cases studied the assailants attempted to induce ejaculation in addition to the typical anal penetration. Most of the rapists had previous records of sexual assault, some also having committed serious nonsexual crimes. A well-founded assumption of the study was that previous imprisonment had some contributory significance, for by far the highest incidence of homosexual rape does occur within prisons.

The "hierarchical sex code" operating in one American prison is examined by Susan Brownmiller in *Against Our Will*. Included is a testimony by Haywood Patterson, the "chief defendant in America's most famous rape case, the Scottsboro affair," in which a group of nine black men allegedly raped two white women. Patterson's account however is of his own prison experience:

> When Patterson landed in Alabama's tough Atmore State Prison Farm in 1937 he was confronted with a cut-and-dried option: either submit to the older men and become a "gal-boy" or defend his bodily integrity and become a "wolf." The issue, as the 25-year-old Patterson saw it, was manhood. He reasoned, "If any of that stuff goes on with me in on it I'll do all the fucking myself. I been a man all my life. . . . "
>
> Patterson's own acid test came early in his stay at Atmore. He had already determined, "If I had to be a part of this life I would be a man," and the first step toward manhood was to patronize the weekend gal-boys. "I called them fuck-boys, I called them all kinds of sorry names. . . . I would say to one of them, 'You come here taking your mommy's and your sister's place, you rotten. . . . ' "
>
> Patterson gradually began to relish his wolf role, but his status had to be periodically defended. In the prison hierarchy there were wolves and bigger wolves. "Even after I had my regular gal-boy it didn't end my troubles with the wolves who wanted to use me that way." A wolf named John Peasely let him know he thought the Scottsboro boy was too young to be a man—"He wanted to use both me and my gal-boy." Patterson went after the older wolf with a switchblade knife, and this event became the turning point of his stay at Atmore. He reported succinctly, "Peasely didn't try to make a girl out of me no more. Nobody did. I had taken a gal-boy, whupped a wolf, and set myself up as a devil."[210]

This account is more than forty years old, but prisons remain the primary setting in which such a hierarchically organized drama of sex and power so clearly takes place. Obvious is the manner in which phallic power and prestige is played out among men without women, but with a more masculine or more feminine fantasy about one another.

Brownmiller quotes Patterson in characterizing a hierarchy of power, but in turning to the amorous prison writings of Jean Genet she is frankly puzzled: "What is a feminist to make of a man who professes to see a compliment in the threat, 'I'd like to give you a shot in the pants,' and who considers a furtive tap on the anus the equivalent of a stolen kiss?"[211] (Brownmiller however ventures no formulation of her own ideal masculine type.) Genet portrays the confounding and surreal ambiance of homosexual love as he experienced it in the prisons and in the depths of his imagination. Genet's passivity is again a lapsing beyond subject and object, an intuition of "pre-natal mass," of the dynamics of Eros on the periphery of consciousness:

> In prison, when the sun that streamed through the window scattered the cell, each of us became more and more himself, lived his own life, and lived it so acutely that we ached, for we were isolated and were made conscious of our imprisonment by the brilliance of the *fête* that dazzled the rest of the world, but on rainy days it was otherwise and the cell was merely a shapeless, pre-natal mass with a single soul in which the individual consciousness was lost. What a sweet feeling when the men of whom it was composed love each other.
>
> At night, I often stay awake. I am the sentinel at the gate of the sleep of others, whose master I am. I am the spirit that hovers above the shapeless mass of dreams. The time I spend there pertains to the time that flows in the eyes of dogs or in the movements of any insect. We have almost ceased to be in the world.[212]

Less poetically but no less psychologically does Genet portray the unifying tendency of a masculine Eros of the lowest common denominator:

> And I feared too the ordeal of the crap can. I knew I could see him there without my love's suffering thereby, but I was not sure I had the physical assurance, the bodily authority, to sit down on it myself without endangering my prestige. In wanting to go to the hole so as to be more deeply buried in abjection—I had the impression of descending when I went there, for my love of Bulkaen made me seek the most nauseating situations for us, perhaps so that we would both be more isolated from the world, just as I lovingly imagined him plunging beneath my covers, releasing his worst odours, making me do likewise so that we would mingle in what was most private about us.[213]

Thus, a sufficient glimpse within what Genet refers to as "a larval world of prodigious richness and violence"—the world of the Great Mother imprisoning the Eros and misting the consciousness of her sons. Sartre described Genet as a "raped child," and in *The Miracle of the Rose* his raped condition has become a prevailing mode of consciousness. Be the victim of rape a woman, a man beaten into submission, or one quite in love with his "gal-boy" status, the loss of bodily integrity is the concrete sign of eroded self-determination, of the invasion of one's inner *temenos*.

Anima-Identification and the Shadow

One image of such an invasion was introduced in chapter six with
an analysand's drawing of anal penetration. This was the man who
dreamed of the "Torture of Rose Marie." Eleven months before the
Rose Marie dream, this same man experienced in a dream the threat
of homosexual violence:

> A dead lion lies on the earth rotting. A woman—the wife of the
> farmer who owns the land—stands nearby and says I may have the
> carcass. Many insects are in the air. At first I hold the big head in
> admiration, noticing its dark lips are segmented in four. I plan to bury
> the big head of the lion in the earth for one year in order to let the
> elements—water, earth, worms, ants, etc.—clean away all the flesh and
> eat the brains out. I then will dig it up and it will be very beautiful—I
> can keep it in my study then. The atmosphere around me is very
> luminous. The skull has fangs like a saber-toothed tiger.
>
> The killer in my boarding house has finally been caught and dis-
> covered to be David Berkowitz [the "Son of Sam"—a New York City
> killer of many young girls who claimed that a 6,000-year-old Egyptian
> demon was dwelling in his neighbor's dog and directed him to kill].
> All of us on the main floor are very relieved and so is a woman like
> Rosemary Spencer, who lived upstairs and was held in such suspicion
> by all of us. I then see the name of the god "Ptah" written on a piece
> of paper.
>
> I piss into an open fountain on the street in front of my shop. Then
> one of a couple of homosexuals comes into my shop. I am immedi-
> ately wary for I know that this guy and his gay lover are killers—they
> were once arrested in California for the ritual slaughter and sexual
> abuse of a bunch of young boys. They are very interested in the
> objects in the shop, and I grow even more afraid. I go to get an old
> classmate and beg him to be with me, talk to me, keep me from being
> alone with the two gay killers. I then run off to a gay bar and ask the
> proprietor to let me call the police with his phone. "You cannot," he
> says. "Well then I'll call an ambulance!" I reply. "All you will get is
> . . . . " I feel trapped. Somebody says something about a gay guy being
> "really loose," and I say, "Well I will be really loose if I don't get the
> hell out of here!" (by *loose* I mean I will get sodomized so severely
> that my anus will get torn loose—torn to shreds!). All the homosexuals
> in the place look at me startled and amused.
>
> I am off in a parking lot waiting for someone. A big green wheel is
> racing around by itself. An older bald man shows up and says of a
> fancy sports car there that all it needs is a pair of spark plugs. I think,
> "AC spark plugs—they will cost only $1.80 and I must get them."
>
> Isis shits out Seth. Seth is red and brown and is important.
>
> In a waiting room a friend shows up. He talks about "incubation."
> He shows me a television commercial in which by means of sublimi-
> nal messages people are instructed about incubation.
>
> I then think of an analyst, and I admire his big blue cubical of
> water.

The alchemical "green lion" devouring the sun (consciousness).
—From *Rosarium philosophorum*, 1550.

Confronted with the dead lion, numerous amplifications come to mind, among them the honey in the head of Samson's lion, and the power symbolically appropriated by Heracles clad in his lion skin. In the dream, it is as if the corpse is released by the mother complex for the purposes of the dream ego. The sustaining strength of some lionlike instinct has gone its natural way into death. The lion often appears as a solar, heroic or kingly creature, figuring in innumerable coats-of-arms to display the power and egoism of the sovereign, as well as being the preeminent beast of the Great Mother. Certainly a possibility-filled image, but in the context of the dream, given the swarm of insects, the mysterious atmosphere surrounding the lion and the process of defleshing which it will undergo, the lion may be taken as an image of the transformative substance in the process of self-transformation. The lion thus images a raging, seizing and devouring instinct, essentially transient and here past its prime.

The fact that the beast is dead by no means implies that the psychic energy sustaining the dream's entire flow of imagery has passed away; quite the contrary, the green wheel whirling around autonomously later in the dream indicates the continuing libido in the transformative symbol. By connecting the natural process of decomposition, exploited here by the dream ego, with the whirling green wheel, the alchemical "green lion" becomes a very appropriate amplification. It is one metaphor for Mercurius, the arcane substance symbolizing the quicksilver movements of the psyche. In alchemy the paws of the raging green lion—as wild and powerful as the bursting sap of green life, as a jungle grasping its prey—are cut off. The lion's hot blood swirls around, forming a container for the primal urge. Psychologically, there is no better image for the heat and containment of "incubation." In the analytic process the paws are cut off through a sacrificial "living-in," the difficult task of reflecting on the instinct instead of acting it out. Given the extremity of the dream as a whole, the fantasy of the saber-toothed tiger is something of an aesthetic flourish, but nevertheless anticipates consciousness (sharp, strong teeth) in the sense of the alchemical dictum, "What Nature leaves uncompleted is perfected through the art."

The dream continues with the irruption of further contents of the unconscious. Similar to the frantic alter ego's realization in the later dream of Rose Marie, the dreamer here finds that he is not alone in his apartment. The wild figure of David Berkowitz has been functioning in him autonomously. A psychotic murderer of women, this man did hold New York in fear for a number of months in 1977. Identifying himself as an agent of a "6,000-year-old Egyptian demon," he is clearly a personification of the "Terrible Male" raging in the equally terrible aspect of the negative Mother—an image of shadow, psychopathy and death. Berkowitz, though far wilder than the black man of the Rose Marie dream, is again related to the dog. One may recall the horrid barking of Cerberos, but also of Hecate and the Erinyes, or the canine figures of Seth and Anubis, the god of the dead. Berkowitz measures his power in the destruction of women. In the striking contrast between the creative, sovereign deity Ptah and the cryptic appearance of Seth—an archetypal image of shadow "created" by Isis—later in the dream, the positive-negative polarity of the archetype of masculine spirit may be seen (as previously explored in chapter five).

At this point in the dreamer's analysis those residents of the apartment building reflected psychic contents more closely related to ego-consciousness. The single woman Rosemary Spencer joins in the mutual relief—her name, appearing here for the first time, coming up eleven months later in the form of Rose Marie. Note that the threat of violation is directed in this dream *not toward a differentiated anima figure,* such as Rose Marie, *but toward the body of the dream ego, indicating the dreamer's continuing identification with the anima.* Such a psychic arrangement is fundamental to the homosexual component of rape.

Resting assured at the capture of the wanted man though the apartment crowd may be, the dreamer has his own shadow to contend with, a task he seems quite unable to take on alone. Of course casually urinating in an outdoor fountain is a rather open invitation to passers-by. The dreamer's display in the shop, like the display of his penis, might give the impression that he "secretly longed to be raped"! Reflected here as well is the characteristic lack of self-containment of the anima-identified man. People whose souls are outside them are often subject to the fantasy that the world has suddenly grown better with the capture of a notorious criminal.

Implicit in the dreamer's running off to a gay bar for help is the homeopathic truth that salvation from a threat lies in the same sector as the threat itself. The homosexuals meet the dreamer's paranoia in an amused way, as if they were the older friends of a jittery young virgin, surprised at her hysterical fears. The threat is finally most anticlimactic, but the essential problem has been fully and emotionally experienced. The green wheel whirls on: a sustained and transforming flow of libido carries the dream onward to an older bald man, vehicle, admired analyst and the clear cube of water. Discernible here is the compensatory movement toward introversion and the deeper reality of the dreamer. "AC/DC" is a slang expression for the contrasting alternation of homo- and heterosexuality (the dreamer's association). His coming-to-terms with the homoerotic aspect of his personality constituted one important element of the analysis.

Whereas David Berkowitz displays unequivocal shadow characteristics for the collective and the dreamer, the homosexuals reflect a dispersion or "latency" of masculinity remaining in the unconscious. Viewed developmentally, this may be imagined as tending toward a further consolidation of the innate masculinity of the personality in its movement away from the mother world. Yet considered structurally, the homosexuals reflect a marked homoerotic side of the dreamer's personality which when rejected quite clearly breeds insecurity, anima-identification, even paranoid ideas, but when contacted may lead to the possibility of a deeper and richer relationship with other men. The dreamer experienced too much fear, however, for this matter to be so nicely concluded. In light of the fact that homosexuality has repeatedly proved to be problematic for rapists so concerned with being "men," the psychological dynamics need to be pursued more deeply.

The Egyptian demon fantasy of David Berkowitz, the peculiar

statement "Isis shits out Seth," as well as the "subliminal message" of the television and the fear of penetration itself, provide a point of departure. The fear of rays from outer space, subliminal messages of control from televisions and other electrical appliances, etc., is standard fare in the symptomatology of paranoid schizophrenia. The paranoia among women concerning rape is widespread, with considerable justification. Fear of rape in prison is another instance. But a more essential and inescapable given is the "prison" of the psyche—the inescapable container of our being, and particularly the single cell of the ego. To the degree that the ego remains rigid, naive or defiantly virginal and unresponsive to the subliminal demands of the individuation process, it is increasingly susceptible to a forceful invasion by the unconscious. In more pathological cases the paranoid succumbs to the fully ambivalent dynamism of, for example, the archetype of Kingship or of the Messiah—witness Charles Manson's doctrine that "total paranoia is total awareness."[214]

The dog-demon commanded Berkowitz to kill women. The Egyptian hieroglyph of the Seth animal is a long-eared jackal-like animal somewhat resembling Anubis, particularly when Seth appears in anthropomorphic form. Seth is a desert prowler, hostile to man, the cause of all moral and physical evil. Famous as he who tricks, dismembers and castrates the sun god Osiris, he is thereby the god of the setting sun. These qualities bring Seth in line with the death of the solar lion early in the dream. As Seth was identified with the night sky, so Horus was with the day, yet this pair of battling brothers jointly hold the ladder by which Osiris ascends to heaven. Jung speaks of Horus as the representative of the true spirit, Seth as an image of bodily instinct. Together, as for instance in the Egyptian image of the human body with the heads of *both* Horus and Seth, they may be seen as the opposites inherent in the essential being of Osiris.[215] In the mythology of Seth, he is more associated with the negative aspect of Isis, in some accounts her brother, the uncle of Horus. One pyramid text also states that Seth once overcame Horus and "treated him like a woman"—this in addition to his murdering and castrating nature. But the specific manner of Seth's appearance in the dream requires further thought. Seth, as "Terrible Male" and exponent of Isis, is her dark creation and active power. What is the meaning of her excreting him in the dream?

Remaining mindful of the fact that all the dream's processes pertain ultimately to the intrapsychic environment of which the body is a major part, "Isis shits out Seth" may be referred initially to the dreamer's own somatic process—or more specifically, to the psychoid unconscious. The maternal matrix of the body is that from which the ego, identifying itself with spirit, emerges and strives for its own

Union of opposites personified as the dual god Horus-Seth. — From Wallis Budge, *The Gods of the Egyptians.*

individual integrity. One may imagine the child in the crib whose ego, a mere germ, is awakened from its deepest *participation* with the maternal uroboros by the ebb and flow of bodily sensations. The uncontrolled excretion of faeces constitutes one primal experience of the autonomous "Other." A consequence of the ego's will to establish control over autonomous forces is that whatever is repressed becomes the personal shadow, which remains intimately related to the maternal unconscious, functioning autonomously as instinctual adversary of the ego.

Freud in his famous Schreber case discussed persecutory delusions and the defense mechanisms posed against them in terms of both somatic and mental dynamics. According to Otto Fenichel, "Schreber attempted through his delusions to protect himself from passive homosexual temptations originating in his infantile attitude toward his father."[216] Here, as in the case of the present dreamer, is uncertainty and ambivalence toward the father concomitant with homosexuality. Freud traces the formation of the persecutory ideation in progression, beginning with the defense against homosexual impulses: "I don't love him, I hate him"; "I don't hate him, he hates me"; "I am justified to hate him for he persecutes me." Fenichel paraphrases Freud in explaining that "the persecution represents the homosexual temptation, turned into a fearful threat, threatening independently of the patient's will."[217] Fenichel cites numerous psychoanalytic papers in which the persecutor, though personified via projection as an actual man, is unconsciously perceived as the patient's own faeces—the sensations of persecution representing intestinal sensations. He continues:

> It is interesting that among the organs projected onto the persecutor, faeces and buttocks play a predominant role. According to Abraham, the process of incorporation in paranoid fantasies is thought of as performed by the anus.[218]

This represents a basic phenomenology of the shadow and the ego's battle with it. It harkens back to the child's primal experience of the complete autonomy of the unconscious as "intestinal sensations"—the alimentary uroboros. Here one may recall the nondifferentiation of Genet and his lover Bulkaen. These dynamics provide additionally a glimpse of the pronounced role of hatred in the maintenance of the ego's sovereignty. The vulgar terms and gestures of abuse with which enemies are identified with the body's posterior and its products emphasize the role of "organs projected" as associated with the shadow. Freud does not leave the matter at this point, however, but speaks of the higher mental functions which he considers sublimations of this somatic base:

Like elements of the body, one's mental characteristics, too, may be projected onto the persecutor. This occurs not only in the projection of the hatred which is basic for the delusion; also certain definite attitudes and expressions, which are ascribed to the persecutor, correspond to traits of the patient and *especially often to the demands of the patient's super-ego....* the persecutor, then, observes and criticizes the patient; the persecutions themselves represent projections of the patient's bad conscience.... The above statements may be summarized in the following symbolic equation: *persecutor = homosexual object = narcissistically hypercathected and projected organ (faeces, buttocks) = projected super-ego.*[219]

Although these dynamics are described with reference to a case of pathological paranoia, the same mechanism, writes Fenichel, "can also be observed in latent homosexual men who are far from being psychotic."[220]

These basic mechanisms of ego defense described in psychoanalytic theory indeed correspond to the dream material of homosexual penetration, the hated split-off part of the personality and the need of help from just this quarter. But their reductive interpretation seems to leave one with conscience as a mere complex and morality reduced to dregs. The stark limitations of Freudian rationalism and literalism were examined in chapter three. The idea of an external superego is ultimately unacceptable in that it begs the question of its own psychic origin; unacceptable as well is the notion that the autonomy of the psyche is reducible to somatic processes for it begs the question of the sustaining form—the unifying "information" or "physical archetype" which sustains the seven- to ten-year replacement of the concrete stuff of the body; and finally unacceptable is the notion that the threatening unconscious contents are merely ego-repressed, incompatible personality traits, for it is inadequate to explain the collective meaning of historical figures such as Seth, Horus or Osiris.

An alternative approach, as presented here, would recognize an irreducible, superordinate personality—the Self—the need for a truly symbolic conception of the body and the creative autonomy of the collective unconscious.

The Initiating Spirit

As the superordinate, regulating center of the personality and archetype of wholeness, the Self encompasses both superego and id, the aerial sovereign and his virgin consort, the "Terrible Male" and his raging mistress, the Great Mother. The primal androgyne of Plato may well be recalled, for besides representing the sexual instinct and "its various relations to its objects," it may be taken as a profound image of the spiritual Self unified in Eros. As the Self is a correlative unity of psychic functions, so also it may be considered as that which sustains the dynamic interplay of dream figures.

In pursuing the relevance of the concept of the Self for the present question of the homosexual component in men and in rape, considerable instruction can be derived from a work by John Layard, "Homoeroticism in Primitive Society as a Function of the Self." In the foreword to this study of peoples in Australia, New Guinea and the New Hebrides, Layard describes the organization of primitive society as an externalization of what we think of as the Self. Just as primitive social structures function hierarchically yet as a unified whole, so the multiple figures in a dream gravitate around a central, unifying axis, the Self.

Layard's article concerns the relationship between men in the cross-cousin marriage system. The young male of the group must surrender a sister and his anima-identification with her, receiving a cousin in return as wife. In those cases where the prospective bride is still young or even unborn, the husband-to-be will take an older brother of the betrothed as his pupil and love partner. The novice taken in this way leaves the world of his mother and joins with an initiating male who, in turn, treats him as the wife/anima-substitute he is, while at the same time leading the novice on toward the man he shall become:

> There is a widespread belief throughout all this area that homosexual intercourse, by which is meant anal intercourse, promotes bodily growth, not only the male sex organs of the junior partner but his whole body. There is a corresponding belief that psychic growth also results from it. It is an aspect of initiation, in this part of the world and at this level of culture, that what is held to be introjected into the boy novice, along with much other cultural influence, is "masculinity" in the form either of actual semen (considered as bodily "food") or of "symbolic semen" said, in initiation, to be introjected anally by the spirits of the ancestors who are the extensions in time (and psychic depth) of the initiating men.[221]

The relationship between homosexuality and the superego described above by Fenichel is immediately apparent. This type of erotic relationship stands as the foundation of the initiation rituals, in which innumerable "hoaxes" are practiced on the novices. In one instance they are placed in a hut as the older men rattle sticks and threaten the youths with anal penetration by the ancestral spirits which they personify. As Layard remarks:

> This may appear to us to be somewhat ludicrous, but to the natives it is of the highest character-forming value. It is a case of the "lowest"

turned into the "highest," for what is actually meant by the "ancestral spirits" (more popularly called "ancestral ghosts") is *the collective spirit of the ancestors* who are the highest cultural and psychical values the natives know. This is the native expression of what we call "conscience," the inner voice that tells a man what is socially right and what he ought to do in spite of possible inclinations to do otherwise.[222]

As one of the natives Layard knew put it:

Where else can the ancestral spirits "come into" the novice's body to initiate him? They cannot come in through the mouth. That is where the mother penetrates with her breast during the boy's infancy. The male influence comes in anally where the man can penetrate, but the woman, who has no organ with which to do so, cannot penetrate.[223]

Clearly the initiatory significance of homosexual penetration may be discerned in the dream presented in the previous section, with a modern-day "male-admiring society" alive in the soul of the dreamer. At the outset the dreamer obtains the lion's carcass from the farmer's wife. Though the negative propensities of the mother—namely death and putrifaction—are cleverly employed, the power of the mother over the dreamer's consciousness is punctuated by her production of Seth and by the homosexual threat. Homosexuality does correlate with the domination of the mother, yet the gay bar is one modern equivalent, however rudimentary, of the primitive men's hut where the phallus is celebrated, and where masculinity seeks its consolidation. The unconscious of the dreamer, similar to the prison or the gay bar, appears to be, to echo Layard's comment on Malekula (New Hebrides), a "men-admiring society, no woman-admiring one, for the men are just beginning to win their independence from the devouring goddess."[224]

In analysis, then, the shadow may manifest as a homosexual rapist. As the phallic exponent of the mother, he is simultaneously a representative of the chthonic aspect of the masculine, and ultimately the initiating spirit. In the dream discussed above, the homosexual ambiance includes the older man with his "AC/DC" suggestion, the analyst and the message of incubation. These dream elements, amplified with the psychoanalytically described dynamics of homosexuality and superego, and joined with Layard's observations on the anal introjection of conscience and culture by the "collective spirit of the ancestors," provide a rich phenomenology of the initiating masculine spirit, its superior ordinance and its significance for the individuation process.

The same analysand recorded a later dream in which he found himself making love with a black man: "I have a huge erection, though I cannot tell if it is mine or the black man's," and a still later

Initiating spirit as dragon.—From Vitruvius, *De architectura,* 1511.

dream in which war had broken out and he and a group of men "were carrying a long, mysterious, radioactive cylinder into a new land as fuel to power the generators of the future." One may reasonably recall the dark and light gods, Seth and Horus, holding the ladder for the ascension of Osiris, and the pyramid text, "Horus strengtheneth and purifieth—Seth strengtheneth and purifieth."

Appropriate to any study of rape that would remain closely related to the mundane deed is the examination of Eros functioning on a low level. The instances of Haywood Patterson and Jean Genet, springing from life situations extremely degraded, serve this end very well. Genet and his lover Bulkaen sharing their private flatulant ambiance form, in Genet's own words, "merely a shapeless pre-natal mass with a single soul in which the individual consciousness was lost." In contrast, the elevated peaks of developed masculine Eros may be observed in the *Symposium* of Plato, or again, in the writings of St. Bernard of Clairvaux. Indeed a virginal soul, St. Bernard "compares himself to the bride who has young maidens who follow her around"—he and his monks, brides of the Spirit:

> He reminds them that whatever he receives from the Lord is also for them, because he loves them. "When I encounter what is hard and austere I confine it to myself . . . what is pleasant and sweet, I share with you. . . . I know that girls are delicate and tender, ill-equipped to endure temptations."[225]

8

Ritual and Sacrifice

Introduction

Sexuality provides the most concrete examples of the erotic will to union. The desire to overcome the separation between subject and object and experience the primal nature of things is, however, a phenomenon at any level of the psychic spectrum from concrete rape to a spiritually informed, ascetic renunciation (which still has a way of employing sexual metaphors, however abstract).

Of crucial importance for consciousness and for the individuation process is the gradual deliteralization and internalization of potential acts through the sacrificial process of reflection. Mythology holds an immense store of imagery by which the various movements of Eros may be pictured. In a discussion of initiation and the "transformation of consciousness about sexuality," James Hillman provides a vivid sense of this diversity:

> Sexuality changes as the Gods who carry its token—the phallus-penis
> —change through life's phases. Pan, Priapus, Hermes, Dionysus, Zeus,
> Apollo, Eros, the Kouroi, Kabeiroi, Sileni, Satyrs, Centaurs—each
> represents a way of initiation into sexual being, each represents a
> fantasy pattern through which the instinct can be experienced. The
> figure of Jesus, both textually and iconographically (with rare excep-
> tions or in disguised form), omits this token altogether. As a result, the
> individual in our culture is given no God-image as an example for the
> initiation into sexual being.[226]

The facts of criminal rape, as well, provide a graphic phenomenology of the movements of Eros. The fantasy or dream of rape, spinning in the psyche of the instinctually driven man, need be approached with a mind both to the actual deed and possibilities and the influence of archetypal patterns which historical and mythological amplifications help one to see.

Hillman emphasizes the dilemma of the sexless Christ for which there is no simple solution. Christianity indeed provides no images by which the erotic side of life can be held closer to consciousness, and no ritual of initiation into this aspect of life. Through the invocation of the divinities of Greek polytheism the symbolic aspects of sexual instincts become psychologically accessible. This provides a desperately needed compensation to the stringent Christian repression which has historically demonized and secularized sexuality. It is

116

true that Christianity arose as a compensation to the old polytheism and the crude instinctuality of many of its rites. There was good reason why Pan became the devil of Christianity. But a categorical repression is finally more destructive than is sustaining in myth and ritual a consciousness of our vital relationship with the sexual gods. This very activity works to preclude the criminal acting-out of sexual instincts, to foster a recognition of the sacred aspect of sexuality and to complement certain shortcomings of Christian dogma.

Maiden Sacrifices to the Underworld

Jung records an interesting legend from the 5th century in which Christianity continued in triumph over the old rites:

> Near the city of Rome there was a certain cavern in which could be seen a frightful and terrible dragon of marvelous size, a mechanical contrivance that brandished a sword in its mouth and had shining red jewels for eyes. Every year girls were consecrated and adorned with flowers, and then given to the dragon in sacrifice. For, as they descended with their gifts, they unwittingly touched the step to which this devilish mechanism of a dragon was attached, and were instantly pierced through with the sword that sprang out, so that innocent blood was shed. A certain monk, who was known to Stilicho the patrician on account of his good deeds, destroyed the dragon in the following manner: he carefully examined each step with a rod and with his hand until he discovered the diabolical fraud. Then, stepping over it, he went down, smote the dragon and cut it to pieces, thus showing that they are not true gods who are made by the hands of men.[227]

This account resembles others which center on sacrifices made to the underworld. In the Greek festival, the Arrhetophoria, honey-cakes and pastries in the shape of snakes and phalli were thrown into the pit "to the mother that she may spare one from death."[228] This gives a distinct picture of the castration fears, fear of the "loss of soul," which the offerings sought to waylay. But recurrent is not only the offering of cakes or phalli, but also of young women:

> There were any number of entrances to Hades in antiquity. Thus, near Eleusis, there was a gorge through which Aidoneus came up and into which he descended after kidnapping the Kore. There were crevasses in the rocks where the souls could ascend to the upper world. ... Similar ideas are suggested by an old Greek custom: girls used to be sent for a virginity test to a cave where there lived a poisonous serpent. If they were bitten, it was a sign that they were no longer chaste. We find the same motif in the Roman legend of St. Sylvester, dating from the end of the fifth century:
> There used to be a huge dragon inside the Tarpeian Hill, where the

capital stands. Once a month magicians and wanton girls went down the 365 steps to this dragon, as though into the underworld, bearing with them sacrifices and purificatory offerings from which the great dragon could be given his food. Then the dragon would suddenly rise up, and though he did not come out he poisoned the air with his breath, so that men died and much sorrow was occasioned by the deaths of children. When, therefore, St. Sylvester was fighting the pagans in defence of truth, the pagans challenged him, saying, Sylvester, go down to the dragon and in the name of thy God make him desist, if only for a year, from this slaughter of human lives.[229]

St. Sylvester then received the miraculous intervention of St. Peter who advised him to chain the doors of the underworld for a millennium.

Jung offers these examples in a discussion of "The Dual Mother," and the battle of the heroic ego to overcome the dread unconscious. Yet he makes the important statement that *"man and dragon might be a pair of brothers, even as Christ identified himself with the serpent."*[230] So once again we see the polarity intrinsic to the archetype of the masculine which has already been considered in Seth and Horus and in terms of the aerial and chthonic poles of the archetype.

But regarding rape, and the sacrificial impulse inherent particularly in its sadistic forms, attention need be given specifically to the fate of the maiden, the anima, in such practices. In the struggle of the ego against its opponent—the "Dual Mother" or the serpentine shadow-brother—a pivotal role is played by her. In this type of legend, a type which Catholic children have perennially found reassuring, the maiden of coming years is neatly rescued. But in rape, of course, there is no question of rescue, and in the emotional experience of a man there can be no simple escape from the fierce ambivalence toward women which may have him in its grasp. It is *the sacrifice of the anima* which constitutes the real archetypal problem, for the sacrifice of the given, transient anima through life amounts to nothing less than the process of emotional maturation. In reality she is deathless, passing on to a new form, a shimmering mirror in which the beast may notice its wings.

The suspicious mechanical dragon in the Roman legend is an example of the excessive, concrete extreme to which sacrificial ritual can be taken—the notion of "religious ritual" rendered farcical by the caprice of scurrilous individuals. Frazer in *The Golden Bough* records numerous instances of virgins offered to water spirits or underworld bogeys, drowned or fed to crocodiles, etc. A common fairytale motif runs: "A certain country is infested by a many-headed serpent, dragon or other monster which would destroy the whole people if a human victim, generally a virgin, were not delivered up to him periodically."[231] Frazer records the following example:

> The Akikuyu of British East Africa worship the snake of a certain river, and at intervals of several years they marry the snake-god to women, but especially to young girls. For this purpose huts are built by order of the medicine-men, who there consummate the sacred marriage with the credulous female devotees. If the girls do not repair to the huts of their own accord in sufficient numbers, they are seized and dragged thither to the embraces of the deity.[232]

Thus the claims of the underworld are satisfied in various ways, but recurrent as the offering is the innocent virgin. However fanciful Catholic legends may be, it would seem that religious ritual, be it Mediterranean, African or any other, inclines in its decadence toward violence and exploitation. In such phases the need for renewal and internal refinement may find personification in such figures as Christ amid the decay of Rome, or Orpheus who transformed and purified the more primitive elements of the Bacchanalia. Similarly, the individuation process, even in the midst of serious regression, tends toward a more conscious relationship with the primitive instinctual levels of the psyche in contrast to a blind immersion in them.

Among the Aztecs, though prisoners of both sexes were sacrificed, women were particularly favored as victims. In a daringly comparative religious study of the mid-16th century, the Mexican Dominican friar Fray Diego Duran describes a series of sacrifices of young women to the goddess Chicomecoatl and other deities. The name Chicomecoatl means "Serpent of Seven Heads"; this she was called "because of the harm she did in barren years, when the seeds froze, when there was want and famine."[233] The second name of the goddess was Chalchiuhcihuatl, meaning "Woman of Precious Stone," used to denote her provision of fertility and abundance. The sacrificial victim was identified with the goddess, robed like the image of Chicomecoatl, and was the center of elaborate ritual of renewal. First, writes Duran, a statue of the goddess was fashioned:

> It was made of wood, carved in the form of a young woman, a maiden some twelve years of age, modelled in the best carving in the land. She was garbed in the native womanly garments, all red, the most splendid attainable. On her head she wore a tiara of red paper upon her cropped hair, which fell to her shoulders. In her ears were incrusted golden earings. On her neck she wore a necklace of golden ears of corn, tied with a blue ribbon. In her hands she held ears of corn, imitated in feather-work and garnished with gold. She held her arms open, like a dancing woman. Her cheeks were colored like those of a woman wearing rouge. This was the usual garb and form of the goddess, who stood in a chamber on the summit of the temple next to

the chamber of the great Huitzilopochtli, all to her greater honor and glory.[234]

Then, in the likeness of this image of Chicomecoatl, "a girl twelve or thirteen years old, the most comely to be found, was chosen to represent this goddess."[235] The girl was presented to the goddess, incensed, greeted with trumpets and conch-shell blasts, had her hair cropped more closely and was carried by the elders bound to a litter. "Thus she was carried in procession into the great courtyard of the serpent wall. She was passed through the end of the hall where Huitzilopochtli stood. *Her passing through this room was the essence of the ceremony.*" Blood offerings from previous sacrifices were presented to her by the priests. The rite culminated after further ritual acts in the following manner:

> When the people had gathered, the girl was offered incense again, no less solemnly than on the previous day. Then she was cast upon the piles of ears of corn and seeds and decapitated. Her blood was gathered in a small bowl, and the wooden goddess was sprinkled with it. All the chamber was sprinkled with it, and so were the offerings of ears of corn, chili, squash, seeds and vegetables which lay there. After her death she was flayed and one of the priests donned her skin. On it were placed all the garments the girl had worn—her tiara on his head, her ears of corn on his neck and hands. He was presented to the public while the drums sounded and all danced, led by the man dressed in the skin of the young girl and the robes of the goddess.[236]

The body of the woman was finally eaten together with those of other sacrificial captives in a feast which, curiously enough, was not considered cannibalistic.

The treatment of the victims in this ritual context displays in full archaic flower a ritualized form of behavior which Groth and Birnbaum found characteristic of the sadistic rapist, including the cropping of hair, keeping of mementoes, washing or cleansing of the body (incense, purification), dressing of the victim in certain ways, forced behavior, cutting and execution, flaying and dismemberment, the religious fantasy and the tendency to appropriate parts or belongings of the victim. Striking is the fact that though the Aztec maiden becomes the personification of the goddess Chicomecoatl, her ritual passage through the great hall of Huitzilopochtli constitutes "the essence of the ceremony." The Aztec priests ritually offer one personification of the goddess, corresponding to the Kore or anima, to a great and terrible personification of the *same* goddess, Chicomecoatl-Chalchiuhcihuatl, yet do so under the ultimate aegis of the supreme masculine deity, "The Lord of Created Things, The Almighty," Huitzilopochtli.

In the sadistic rapist's immersion in criminal passion, as in the brutally achieved, liminal state of the Aztec priests, psychic opposites are superceded. This is achieved in the Aztec ritual by the donning of the woman's skin—an image of androgyny—whereby one is reunited with the mother and with the collective unconscious. Indeed, precisely this type of ceremony was exploited in a florid anima fantasy by D.H. Lawrence in "The Woman Who Rode Away." Lover of women though he may have been, his emphasis falls finally on the male and the raging masculine spirit. As his character is offered up, Lawrence makes a stark observation which amounts to a warning: "Then the old man would strike, and strike home, accomplish the sacrifice and achieve the power. The mastery that man must hold, and that passes from race to race."[237]

There are, we must now emphasize, corresponding contents in the individual, contemporary psyche. Periodically the psychologically inadequate, "virginal" structure of consciousness must be offered up and renewed in the forward flow of the individuation process. The ego seems forever naive to what is secretly transpiring, though dreams such as the following (by the same man who dreamt of the rotting dead lion and later of Rose Marie) may make a considerable impact:

There is brewing political chaos both between Russia and the United States, and between blacks and whites who would butcher one another. I see an old dining room like in my grandmother's place years ago—there is an eerie tree, an image of a tree cast up against the sky through the windows. It is colorful and has many stars.

A child is being born—it is on an escalator which goes up and down at the same time. My father is there, he is like my wife and my brother. He is dead and alive, or as *though* dead—he wobbles around incoherently. He is giving birth to the child ("He" being my father, my wife, my brother, indistinguishably.) He has a large vagina and a big ugly belly. He can hardly stay awake, hardly care for the child who is at this point in a very critical passage. The child might die! I rub oil on the clitoris of this father-wife-brother. There are tubes going into the child—his lungs might burst from this . . . No, he's safe —there is madness.

I am the functionary of a Dracula-like madman, a kind of spiritual rapist, who is in my mother's bed in a totally black room. There is a woman whom he is intent on claiming, on making insane and endlessly psychotic. His face is gore and blood and darkness. I am taking care of the woman for him—Mrs. X [a mental patient]. Her face is filled with a deep and uncomprehending terror. I and the madman seek to totally claim women's souls. I hold this woman at the top of the stairway in my apartment. I see, as I look into her face, that her pupils are tiny swirling pools of blood. She is on her back and I take a small silver needle, pierce her left pupil and stir around and around in the tiny ocean of blood. I then throw the woman—but there are really

6, 7 or 8 of them now—down the stoney stairway into blackness and
to the madman.

I then become aware that someone will be killed and descend into
the darkness as the sun rises. Then there is a green living snake which
is made of plastic with wine inside. The snake is somehow there as a
complement to the child.

I am then making love with a cute young nurse. But then, out in
front of my childhood home with my wife and her mother...an
immense boa constrictor with a penis-head comes up toward me. I hit
this creature on the head. Crazy animals are running around. Then I
am going somewhere with my most-loved uncle and his wife. He is
naked and has as a scrotum the huge bag of a cow. It is covered with
nipples and has a big scar on it. I must then care for that child, for it
is urinating all over.

Many features of this dream are by now familiar: rape clearly as
a matter of the soul, the apocalyptic chaos of war and destruction as
was seen in the case of Charles Manson, the ambivalent simultaneity
of the fear and persuasive power of black Eros, as well as the anima
image which reflects it. The entire sequence takes place close to the
Great Mother and the shadow—the mental patient, Mrs. X, being an
appropriately mad anima image to reflect an instinctual Eros of
corresponding quality.

The first segment of the dream centers on the grandmother's
home which, though rather prosaic in itself, points to a background
in the Great Mother. The brewing political chaos on her broad plain
signals the activity of the terrible aspect of the mother. Interest
focuses on the archetypal aspects of the dream, for the nature of the
"eerie tree" points beyond the prosaic and personal to the universal.
Typically, when ego-consciousness is threatened with chaos, an archetypal image of an eternally new world is simultaneously offered
by the unconscious. The axial tree is here joined by the image of the
up-down escalator (Jacob's ladder!) which transports the nascent
child. The child is the beginning and the end, wounded by incarnation yet whole by proximity to the archetypal world, created and
uncreated, androgynous—a cry of new life.[238] Striking in the dream
is the child's uncertain yet "just so" parentage—an amalgam of
father, brother and wife—but precisely a stuporous, alive/dead, geni-
tally female father in labor, with a bulging uterine belly.

Since femininity and familial incest provide the matrix of birth,
the child signals an extraordinarily creative bonding of the masculine elements of the personality. The role of the father recalls the
initiatory rebirth rituals ubiquitous in primitive societies through
which the novice passes from the mother world to the "men's hut."
Many such rites of passage correspondingly include circumcision, the
older men feeding or even providing walking and talking lessons for

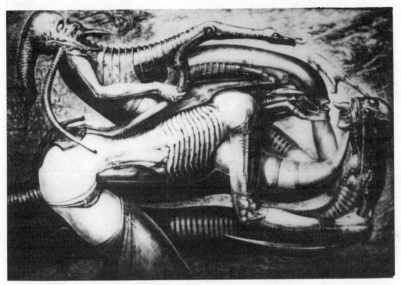

"Necronom V," the underworldly union of Eros (Life) and Death, by
Swiss artist H.R. Giger.—From *Necronomicon.*

the "child," the display of ritual accoutrements, esoteric instructions,
etc. The uncle, with his cowlike scrotum, carries a similar significance—a nurturing maternal male. In light of the fact that the uncle,
as well as the father, was in reality deceased, there is a feeling of the
return of the chthonic spirits of the dead, or as Layard has described, "the collective spirit of the ancestors."

Wife, father, brother, uncle—but what of the Dracula-like madman? The dreamer's father had been a persona-identified man in
the extreme—a protestant Pentheus desperately bent on maintaining
a rationalist and self-compromising world-view. Of course he had an
immense shadow problem. The "spiritual rapist" amounted to a
family secret and, for the analysand, a crucial figure along the back
road to maturity. The demonic figure has all the characteristics well
known from the horror films—Dracula, Bluebeard, or more recently
the "Alien" created by H.R. Giger for the film of that name. He is
the personification of a furious depth of life which is indistinguish-
able from death.

As the dream opened the opposing psychic forces image themselves in a dispersion of warring factions, in many ways as psychically distant as the starry sky. Through the dreamer's waking reflection on his role in the dream as the shadow's·functionary, the

dynamism of the impersonal depths becomes *a uniquely personal experience,* a responsibility born of personal involvement. As the erotic current of the dream "escalates" psychic consciousness toward new life in parent and child, likewise it affords the opportunity for the dreamer to "achieve" *lower consciousness.* The lower realm not only needs to be reflected on the surface, it also needs to acquaint daytime perspectives with its depths.

The madman is the only anonymous figure in the dream, first appearing in the mother's bed in the dark and then in the blackness at the foot of the stairs. Once more the imago of the personal mother appears as the gateway to the unconscious. The dreamer performs a decidedly apotropaic ritual, yet with a lunar insight, when he pierces the eye of the psychotic woman, who then proves to be the true intermediary—the sacrificial offering. Mrs. X, though a daytime acquaintance, has borderline whirlpool eyes, human and superhuman qualities. She seems to be an anima image fading along a spectrum from the innocent Rose Marie to the queen of the underworld herself, bride of Hades.

Psychotherapeutically, one climbs up and down the axial tree, sacrificing one's bloody innocence and naive madness at the perilous threshhold. In the process the integrity of the personality is protected and renewed in ritual experience of the archetype—integration and dis-integration, aversion and attraction precluding blind possession. It is little wonder that analysis is a strictly private affair. The deepest criminal impulse and the highest religious impulse appear to be as ultimately akin as Christ and the Devil.

The ritual piercing of the eye in fact amounts to a frightened attempt to avert the Evil Eye. One famous instance of the malignant eye is the joint possession of one eye by the three Gorgons. Jane Harrison states that the Evil Eye was itself not commonly portrayed in Greece. "But the prophylactic Eye, the eye set to stare back the Evil Eye, is common on vases, on shields and on the prows of ships."[239] She reproduces a Roman mosaic placed in the entrance of a merchant's home. Its inscription reads:

> "God may be propitious to those who enter here and to the Basilica of Hilarius," and to make divine favor more secure, a picture is added to show the complete overthrow of the Evil Eye. Very complete is its destruction. Four-footed beasts, birds, reptiles attack it, it is bored through with a lance, and as a final prophylactic, on the eyebrow is perched Athene's little holy owl. Hilarius prayed to a kindly god, but deep down in his heart was the old savage fear.[240]

Previously encountered as "strongly for the father," Athene is also an image of the virginal integrity of the soul against Gorgons, hydras, chthonic bogeys and the like. Perhaps the piercing lance is

Athene's, as the silver needle of the dream suggests a protective silver moonbeam from the far hemisphere of the anima. Only the lunar is a match for lunacy, and the blood-swirling eye claims no victim save the woman abducted into darkness—one of those maidens "doomed to die."

As in the passing of Rose Marie, there is no end. The death below synchronizes with the rising of the new sun in mythic symmetry. But the green snake also rises. The appearance of the wine-filled snake as a "complement to the child" is an essential detail. Jung's remark that "man and dragon might be a pair of brothers, even as Christ identified himself with the serpent," may be recalled as the child and the snake come together in the dream—just as the instinctual Seth and the spiritual Horus personify the opposites inherent in Osiris. The stuporous fat-bellied man of the dream suggests the satyr Silenus, foster father of Dionysos. As if Silenus were truly lending Dionysian instruction, the green snake, though rather artificially plastic, is alive with wine, while the earlier fear for the child was that "his lungs might burst," presumably with too much air, i.e., spirit. Thus the wine-filled snake would compensate for too little sense of the Dionysian.

This dreamer is of protestant Christian background. Recalling his preoccupation with "maturity," which he conceived patriarchally in terms of ego development, the child may be seen as a one-sided constellation more related to the ego—particularly since the dreamer knew the child, father, wife and brother personally. The snake appears only *after* the fierce experience as shadow's functionary, and after the descent of the woman. Hence enthusiasm at the birth of the "divine child" at this juncture would be sorely misplaced. The psyche goes right ahead in reflecting both the eternal concomitant of ego-development, namely hate, and simultaneously the saving connection of the ego-identified personality with its instinctual pole.

The dream concludes with recapitulations of the same desire and defense. The "most-loved uncle" with his maternal aspect and his ease promises further nurture and, given his wound, sober instruction. The child consists quite naturally of flesh and blood, and presses upon the dreamer the mundane responsibilities of psychological maturity and inner paternity.

Sacrifice and Consciousness

The archetypal perspective of sacrifice is but one possible approach to the problem of rape. The phallic deities, as we have seen, offer numerous ways in which the movements of Eros may be imaged. However, sacrifice may be considered as the fundamental perspective in that sacrifice represents par excellence the regulatory and transformative activity of the Self. It is also particularly appropriate to younger men who actually do commit the crime of rape as a means of asserting their masculinity. Following rape to its extreme, for instance in the sadistic rape-murder, its deep sacrificial impulse may best be discerned. This leads directly to the central question of what it is that is sacrificed in the destruction of the woman.

As is known, the rapist is a weak, impotent, angry and depressed individual compensating for just these deficiencies with fantasies and demonstrations of virility, power and possession. His battle is with forces of the unconscious with which he is unable to deal internally. Although the figure of the young woman—the Kore anima—has been dealt with by allusion to mythological images, the rape victim may be anyone so long as she figures as the carrier of masculine projections. Typically there is a rift—founded upon the archetypal contrast between mother and daughter—in which the negative aspects of the feminine, though profoundly unconscious from the start, are further overlaid with the repression of maternal qualities which the male seeks to divorce from the erotic object. She is imagined as the possession of the man even as he himself becomes progressively more possessed by the pervasively feminine unconscious.

The victim of sexual assault, her beauty or plainness irrelevant, is thus appropriated by the egoistic claims of the male; the fact that rapists have even been known to call again or propose marriage is startling confirmation of this point. But, as Jung has stated, "the unknown in man and the unknown in the thing fall together in one."[241] The unconscious male dread of the feminine and the fantastic power of the unconscious are precisely this unknown which Jung describes. In the act of rape the ambivalence of the feminine comes into its own; the rapist, like Hades, becomes the masculine intermediary of one profound constellation over which the Earth Mother presides. Yet simultaneously the archetype of the masculine is seeking its broader constellation in the personality of the rapist through sacrifice.

At this level, of course, the dynamics of sacrifice are so rudimentary as to scarcely warrant the term. Recalling the deeds of the sadistic murderer Eric, for instance, one sees a "piece of unalloyed naturalism, banal, grotesque, squalid, horrifying and profound as nature herself." With these words Jung described the sacrificial vision of the 3rd-century Greek alchemist, Zosimos, as it contrasts with the ritual sacrifice of the Catholic Mass.[242] Unquestionably worthy of the same adjectives is the picture which the sexual offender places before the mind. In the visions of Zosimos the sacrifice and the sacrificer are one and the same. In like manner, no conception of the unitary psychic phenomenon of rape and sacrifice can be attained by remaining with the external facts. Once again the psyche may speak for itself, as in this dream of the same analysand whose material was discussed in the previous section:

> I am in Africa with a woman I know. The landscape is dotted with the corpses of black people, dead and rotting in the sun . . . it's all quite natural.
>
> Two "primitives"—two men—have a one-half pig, one-half woman creature which they hold firmly and bind. At first I think this is some kind of rape, but it turns into a kind of sacrifice. One of the men chops off one foot of the creature and blood spurts strongly out forming a swirling circular pattern.
>
> Then the scene changes and a philosopher is behind me laughing. I see a kind of stage set being prepared. . . . I am in motion. . . . the stage is made in a symmetrical way and in very beautiful colors. Jacob has something to do with the production. . . . I am moving along. . . .

The dream opens on a plain in Africa, a Great Mother indeed, surging with life and death, "all quite natural." The dreamer associated the woman/pig creature with a somatic fantasy he had had about the backside of his body as feminine, his anus corresponding to the vagina. The philosopher was a man he knew and respected, while Jacob had clearly figured throughout the analysis as a shadow figure. The woman companion at the beginning of the dream he knew and regarded as terribly naive—an aging virgin. Pertinently enough, the young man had previously dreamt of this woman walking down the street while he, flying above in the form of a falcon (Horus), imagined seducing her "in a gentle manner." Simultaneously a sinister rapist had been stalking her on the ground. Recalling a similar dissociation in the dream of Rose Marie, one may assume in the image of the "naive" acquaintance not only the dreamer's own naiveté concerning the sinister and deadly aspects of his nature, but also the provisional sense of comfort afforded by just such a harmless and unassuming female companion. In the falcon dream both personifications of the masculine were centered on this innocent anima figure. In the above dream the two "primitives" join not in a simple rape or seduction but in a ritual sacrifice. The strange amalgam of anonymous woman and pig reflects the psyche's spontaneous shift away from the concrete biological life of the mother toward a symbolic perspective—a movement through sacrifice to *psychic* life.

The dismemberment of the woman/pig spurts a powerful circle of blood and brings in its train the symmetrical theater and a rainbow of colors. The destruction of the sacrificial creature spells a moving-on to new enclosure, and the possibility of a more comprehensive "theater" for the conscious experience and containment of emotional life. A colleague reports of working analytically with a middle-aged Don Juan who secretly scorned and feared women. A decisive dream of the analysis consisted of himself and a shadow figure raping a young woman on a staircase. The dream forced him to accept his unconscious, negative feelings toward the women he had consciously idealized. The movement of the present dream likewise brings the dream ego into an intimate and inescapable relationship with his own shadow. This constitutes an essential trimming of the falcon-ego's wings—a symmetrical balancing of the personality.

But what of the laughing philosopher? Admired and respected as this man was, his laughter at the ostensibly terrible sacrifice is as enigmatic as the appearance of the analyst and Dr. Spock in the dream of Rose Marie. The pursuit of this question leads to the heart of the problem of rape and its transformation through sacrifice.

First, it is no coincidence that the sacrificial creature is a combination of woman and pig, for "the killing of the boar is the oldest symbol we know for the killing of the Great Mother's son-lover."[243] The boar was the replacement for Adonis in his sacrificial rites, and as a compensatory opposite, in Greece suckling pigs were sacrificed as Persephone to the underworld in the course of the Eleusinian mysteries, "symbolizing the sacrifice of her young 'innocent' virginity."[244] In Malekula boars received for sisters given in the cross-cousin marriage system serve as the native's sole sacrificial animal. Mother as well as sisters are strictly taboo precisely because they personify the natural and instinctual realm toward which the libido of the male regressively inclines. As Layard says of the Malekulan Maki ritual, and of sacrifice in general:

> The sacrificial animal fulfills the function of an *alter ego*, which in the initial period of his relationship with it he first rears as a woman would rear a child, then consecrates, cherishes and adores it, thereby investing it with his own secret and cherished primitive desires which, as we shall see, have no other outlet and would otherwise destroy him with their total demands.[245]

Meeting this statement with rape in mind, one might seek to imagine the rapist's fantasy of woman, elaborated and cherished in daydream, in masturbatory ritual, in the fantasy of powerful sexual acts which she would welcome and enjoy; and recall simultaneously the alienation, the sentimental and vicious ambivalence for "she" who has not yet understood. In the following passage Layard well describes the *participation mystique* of individuals in primitive society and the spiritual "principle that intrudes." The sacrificial current which would transform the incestuous *prima materia* of rape in the contemporary psyche may be conceived likewise.

Participation mystique (a sense of one-ness or identification) is what is symbolized by "incest," whether physical or psychological. This problem is a dual one, since the feminine principle is itself dual, at first life-giving and then devouring. But the ritual of sacrifice reverses all this, first destroying in order then to transform, thus bringing about in spirit the rebirth of what was simultaneously being renounced in the flesh. Externally and from the mythological angle, what all this Maki ritual is concerned with is the devouring aspect, the mother wanting to devour her son . . . and, in reverse, the son wanting to devour his mother; also the brother wanting to deprive the sister of her virginity, and so, symbolically, to "devour" her.

The opposite principle that intrudes itself into the scene to prevent this is that of psychic masculinity—not biological masculinity which will take all it can, but psychical masculinity, here represented by the father who, with the jealousy of the husband regarding his wife, and of the father regarding his daughter, stands between man and his incestuous desires and represents the transforming principle. It is the father who symbolizes for the son that son's own inner masculinity, the principle that turns hypothetical animal man into human being and lays the foundation of society and at the same time of spiritual life and inner development. It is also the same principle of restraint that creates friendship between men.[246]

As the consciousness- , conscience- and culture-making spirit of the father principle (be this considered as superego, ancestral spirits or as the archetype of the wise old man) presides over the homoerotic initiation, likewise this principle of masculine spirit ultimately represents the prime exponent of sacrifice. Exactly this significance may be observed in the appearance of paternal figures in the dream material discussed: in the dream of Rose Marie—the analyst, the poet and Dr. Spock as well as the unseen author of the "curse"; in the dream of the threatening gay bar—the morally indignant uncle, the older man and the analyst; in the dream of the pig/woman sacrifice—the laughing philosopher. In the dramatic dream of the Dracula-like madman, the dreamer himself appears as the sacrificing figure. Perhaps most clearly exemplary in its reflection of the archetype of the masculine's role in sacrifice, the dream ego performs the ritual in a highly numinous atmosphere and, as is an essential characteristic of sacrifice, *in intimate, simultaneous relationship with the forces of consciousness and the archetypal shadow.* In this way we are granted a sense of the archetype's full range and the numinosity of its vortex.

The fact remains, and a completely archetypal fact it is, that the entire process of transformation takes place, or is enacted, vis-à-vis the ultimate "Other"—the archetype of the feminine. The male attitude toward the feminine is wholly relative to the degree to which the masculine ego-consciousness has differentiated itself from the primal matrix of the unconscious. This development unquestionably consists in the establishment of ego sovereignty through the will to power. This is an essential prerequisite which enables the person to turn and face the psychic background of consciousness. Prematurely undercutting the fantasized "sovereignty of the ego" in theory or in practice can easily effect a repression of the power problem. Only an ego orientation of some minimal self-possession can thereafter be changed through sacrificial reflection.

Although sacrifice as an archetypal process goes on within the psyche be it reflected or unconscious, Jung is emphatic in pointing out that in the truest sense "sacrifice only takes place when we feel the self actually carrying it out on ourselves,"[247] for "unconscious self-sacrifice is merely an accident, not a moral act."[248] The destructive acts of the rapist, murderer and, most clearly, the suicide represent just such an unconscious play of the archetype of sacrifice. Recall the world as a woman's thought for Charles Manson; the white woman as "Ogre" for Eldridge Cleaver; the women tortured, skinned, killed and inseminated post-mortem by the sadistic rapist Eric; the virgins offered to the monsters of the underworld in Greece and Rome; the Aztecs donning the skin and eating the corpse of the beheaded woman; the pathetic adolescent killer Allesandro Serenelli; the emotions and defensive violence of the clinical rapist; as well as the dream material we have discussed. All this is the background and evidence for considering rape as an initially propitiatory but potentially transformative act.

Jung states that "the annual sacrifice of a maiden to the dragon is perhaps the ideal sacrifice on a mythological level. In order to mollify the wrath of the Terrible Mother the most beautiful girl was sacrificed as a symbol of man's concupiscence."[249] As has been seen, these maidens pass away in accordance with their fate within a pervasively feminine constellation. Reflection on the instinctual drive which hastens the passage of these transient forms of the anima requires a strict *ritual control;* thus it may lead to an initiation into psychic consciousness.

Greek Maiden Sacrifices

Within our own tradition, Greek sacrificial rituals and the tales surrounding them provide useful and imaginative instruction regarding the ritual control of archetypal forces. Jane Harrison distinguishes two major types of Greek sacrifice, one being a ritual of "tendence" devoted to the Olympians, "a joyous thanksgiving to the gods who are all white and bright, beneficent, of the upper air." This type included a festive shared meal, while a second type of sacrifice consisted of a surrendering to "those below, who are black and bad and malignant," in which the offering was wholly destroyed.[250] The second type were rituals of "riddance" and "aversion"—a "holocaust, a sacrifice without a feast":

> The dread ceremonial . . . in its crudest, most barbarous form, is very clearly shown on the vase-painting . . . from a "Tyrrhenian" amphora now in the British Museum. The scene depicted is the sacrifice of Polyxena on the tomb of Achilles. In the *Hecuba* of Euripedes, Neoptolemus takes Polyxena by the hand and leads her to the top of the mound, pours libations to his father, praying to him to accept the "soothing draughts," and then cries,
> "Come thou and drink the maiden's blood
> Black and unmixed."
> In the center of the design . . . is the omphalos-shaped grave, which is in fact the altar. Right over it the sacrifice takes place. Neoptolemus, as next of kin to the slain man, is the sacrificer; Polyxena, as next of kin to the slayer, is the sacrifice. The ghost of the slain man drinks her blood and is appeased, and thereby the army is purged.[251]

In this example the *omphalos* is ritually and symbolically interchangeable with a more common form of low altar—contrasting with the raised altar used in honoring the Olympians—known as the *eschara*. This low altar is "a trench in the earth," where offerings are made "to those who are gone below," "to heroes or to the dead."[252] Polyxena is darkly clad, and typically animals offered as surrogates for the suppliants were black. The chthonic ritual was usually nocturnal, and victims were characterized by a word which in Latin is *sphagion* (plural *sphagia*) meaning "a thing slaughtered."[253]

> The word explains itself: it is not the sacrifice burnt, not the sacred thing killed and carved for a meal, but the victim hacked and hewn to pieces. . . .
> It is interesting to note in this connection that the word is always used of human victims, and of such animals as were used as surrogates. The term is applied to all the famous maiden sacrifices of mythology. Ion asks Creousa:
> "And did thy father sacrifice thy sisters?"
> And Creousa with greater ritual precision makes answer:
> "He dared to slay them as sphagia for the land."[254]

Though victims of both sexes, and animals most frequently of all, have been offered in times of famine, pestilence or battle throughout historical times, our central concern here is the sacrifice of women. As Harrison has shown, women were offered in the ritual aversion of chthonic deities in connection with the cult of the hero, and, as *sphagia*, completely destroyed. Now, in pursuit of the phenomenology of maiden sacrifice we shall briefly examine the stories of Dirke, Makaria, Alcestis and Iphigenia, all famous examples of our theme in heroic mythology. The fate of each one provides a useful image of the archetypal pattern involved in the individual's sacrifice of the anima.

The first story concerns Amphion and Zethos, founders of the seven gates of Thebes and sons of the famously beautiful Antiope, lunar woman and lover of Zeus. Amphion, musical and contemplative, and Zethos, active and warlike, were unlike many fraternal pairs in their lack of hostility toward one another. After many years of separation from Antiope, they meet her again on the very day when Amphion has for once decided to join the hunt of his brother Zethos. That day their erstwhile mother, broken and scarcely recognizable, had just escaped from the slavery of Queen Dirke, who had gone off as a maenad to worship Dionysos but now appears in a frenzy and commands the brothers to bind Antiope to a bull that she be dragged to destruction. Enlightened of their mother's identity by an old herdsman, "the brothers ran after the woman, freed Antiope, caught Dirke and bound her to the bull. The queen was consequently dragged to death."[255] Queen Dirke's body was burned and the ashes strewn into the spring of Ares. The pure water of the Theban spring and brook was thereafter called Dirke, which means "spring."

The motif of the spring also appears in the story of Makaria, "blessed one." "The tale ran in Athens, a virgin must die to get the victory; Persephone would have that offering."[256] At a moment of military crisis, Makaria, daughter of Heracles, volunteered to be sacrificed. "On the spot where she was offered up a spring arose, which preserved her name for the future," and likewise the spring at Marathon was in her honor known as "a fountain of blessedness."[257]

In the myth of the death of Alcestis, wife of Admetus (meaning "unsubduable," an appellation also of the king of the underworld), the Moirai, goddesses of Fate, had extended to Admetus a life twice as long on condition that someone die for him on the original day of his end. Alcestis, the volunteer, is brought to a grave where Death would take her forthwith, were Heracles not there to battle him. As Neumann points out in discussing the theme of the "marriage with Death":

> Alcestis was a Kore-Persephone, a goddess of death and the under-
> world, whose husband Admetus was originally the indomitable Hades
> himself. . . . she belonged to the group of the great matriarchal Pheraia
> goddesses who reigned in the primordial age of Greece. It was only in
> the course of historical development that the goddess Alcestis became
> the "heroine" and her divine husband the mortal king Admetus, a
> typical example of secondary personalization in which originally ar-
> chetypal elements are reduced to a personal level.[258]

Our final mythical example, the story of Iphigenia, provides a still broader context for the sacrifice of the maiden. The superhuman nature of Iphigenia is immediately apparent on account of her birth as the daughter of Theseus and Helen,[259] though she is most familiar to us as the first-born and most beautiful daughter of Agamemnon and Clytemnestra. The situation of her "death" is once again war, at a time when bad weather has hampered the naval operations of Agamemnon's troops. While contemplating the sacrifice of a dappled fawn to Artemis, Agamemnon errs in saying, "Not even Artemis herself...."[260] His impious slip of the tongue instantly counteracts his intended sacrifice of the fawn and renders him insolent before the goddess. The wind fails altogether. Kalchas, the military diviner, reveals that Agamemnon's eldest daughter must be sacrificed to appease the divine offense. Kerényi continues the story:

> But how would Klytaimnestra yield up her daughter to be a victim? Odysseus is said to have thought of the lie: Iphigeneia was to come to Aulis to marry Achilles. Marriage and death, as in the famous lament of Oedipus' daughter, were always associated ideas, ever since Hades carried off Persephone....
>
> But Iphigeneia was not dragged by her fair hair to the sacrifice. A wall-painting of Pompeii shows us Odysseus and Diomedes lifting her up in their arms and carrying her to the altar. The saffron-dyed dress which girls who served Artemis at Brauron used to wear slipped off her, her bosom lay bare to the knife. Agamemnon turned away and covered his face. She stretched out her arms to the goddess. Kalchas, the sacrificial priest, however, now saw what was coming. Artemis watched over the scene and showed her power to save, which Agamemnon had doubted. At the very moment of the killing she substituted a hind for the girl and carried Iphigeneia through the air to the Tauric Peninsula... to serve as her priestess among the barbarians. Human beings were sacrificed to her there.... These the priestess had to take possession of for the goddess, who there was named Parthenos — that is, Maiden — or actually Iphigeneia, who enjoyed such inhuman worship. Yet Iphigeneia was to find her Greek home again on Attic soil, at Brauron, as a heroine in the service of Artemis and her *alter ego*.[261]

Female figures such as Polyxena, Makaria, Alcestis and Iphigenia are thus offered at the behest of men in sacrificial actions informed by the gods. Typically this takes place at a critical moment of crisis for consciousness—in war on a collective level, or amid warring opposites in the individual psyche. Dirke's end results more from the wild actions of mere boys, but nevertheless corresponds. The dream of the Dracula-like madman, the psychotic woman and the nascent child began, it will be recalled, with "a brewing political chaos," with blacks and whites clashing and "an imminent threat of war" between Russia and the United States. Similar material, so common in dreams, was a major component of the apocalypse fantasy of Charles Manson, whose followers were involved in blood sacrifice. Reflected in each case is a "global" tension in the personality, owing to its having become, and remained, in a state of maladjustment through brittle ego-identifications and instinctual *participation*—a situation the psyche as a whole can no longer tolerate.

In such an impasse, where the reconciling and integrating function of the gods, i.e., the collective unconscious, need be recognized and invoked lest it come into play in a completely unconscious and autonomous fashion (such as rape exemplifies), sacrifice alone can effect a transformation. A defiant resistance or an overly surrendering attitude both may miss the demand for a conscious, reflective participation in the necessary deed. Just as any individual personality has its archetypal counterpart in the sphere of the gods, so dream figures such as Rose Marie, the psychotic woman with her eyes of blood, or the pig/woman, who are sacrificed and "destroyed," are in the last analysis transient guises of man's female soul complex, the anima, which changes its face according to the level of consciousness. In her role as alter ego of the goddess, Iphigenia, like the female personification of the Aztec Chicomecoatl, stands out prominently in her immortality.

Despite the unusual lack of hostility between Amphion and Zethos, the competitive antagonism between two brothers is a common archetypal theme in heroic mythology. On an individual level it corresponds to the tension between ego and shadow and polarized psychic functions (thinking/feeling, intuition/sensation, and intraversion/extraversion). Both the sons, Amphion and Zethos, are bound unconsciously to their unrecognizeable mother Antiope. The day in which the musical and contemplative Amphion chooses to join the hunt of his wilder brother ends with the destruction of the ostensibly wicked Dionysian Queen Dirke. In defending their mother, lover of the Olympian Zeus, the "terrible woman" is compulsively destroyed by the brothers' own bullish instinctuality. They are caught between disparate images of the feminine, with the brothers' very compatibility underscoring their unconsciousness. Actually the bull images their joint shadow more than they mirror one another's. Had the brothers heard a later version of their own story, in which Zeus in the form of a satyr makes love with their dear mother, their shared fantasy might have been sorely disrupted! Their victim Dirke nevertheless proves her immortal essence through fire and ashes as a spring of pure water. One may recall the unending music composed of Rose Marie's cry and the harpsichord, the endless story of de Sade's whores, Scheherazade in the *1001 Nights,* the grace known to

Serenelli, Cleaver or Apuleius' Lucius. From the passing of one youthful form of the anima springs a fount of renewal, be she Dirke, Makaria or any other.

Iphigenia in her Pompeian portrayal possesses an uncanny knowing and trust in her divine career. Agamemnon shrinks aghast from the necessary deed, as Abraham, knife in hand, must also have anguished. However inferior women were held to be in Greece or whatever historical precedents our stories recall, one is psychologically compelled to accept the necessity of the sacrifice. Ironically, the outrageous manifestation of the masculine will to sovereignty in the slaughter of the maiden, is ultimately the very sign and seal that this will to power is insufficient and that the masculine is insufferably polarized and alone. One need recall that the state of consciousness had become a chaos of opposing factions, imaged as clashing armies. The impasse reached, the goddess is recognized as the only solution —offering a possibility of experiencing a more complete state of things. She is the matrix of renewal. The rigid hubris of ego-consciousness, as in Agamemnon's doubting, means outright provocation; the insufficient development of consciousness as seen in Amphion and Zethos means being swamped by the instinctual unconscious. But possessing an eye for two worlds is Kalchas the diviner and priest. He "saw what was coming" and understood the nature of the goddess.

The Union of Masculine and Feminine

The spiritually-identified heroic ego and its instinctual twin, be it personified anthropomorphically as shadow figure or theriomorphically as dragon or serpent, have been recognized as a polar unity within the archetype of the masculine. In discussing the hero as a mythical personification of the ego, and referring to the transformation of ego-consciousness, Jung points out that "the essence and motive force of the sacrificial drama consist in an unconscious transformation of energy, of which the ego becomes aware in much the same way as sailors are made aware of a volcanic upheaval under the sea"[262]—tidal wave!

For all the control over his place in the world or over "his woman" which the rapist or any man might wish to possess, his ego remains but one chamber in a house of indeterminable expanse. Brownmiller has a chapter entitled "The Myth of the Heroic Rapist," in which she explores the lush growth of popular fantasy that maintains the notion of the rapist as a capricious, glamorous toughguy. But the fantasy of rape as an avenue of the individuation process is heroic only in so far as ego-consciousness comes to a tacit and sober acceptance of the full "burden of destiny and suffering" characteristic of the true Greek hero.[263] For the sacrifice must ultimately be oneself. Kerényi points out that in contrast to the banal popular image of fairytale heroes, those absurd champions, "the mythology of Greek heroes, although it is equally concerned with god-men and with foundations, is characterized by the fact that its emphasis, its peculiar stress, is laid on the side of the *human*"; and further, that in heroic mythology "the human importance lies in the traditional stories which had their cult for a background."[264] Clearly in our examples of such traditional stories, of the *sphagia,* of the blood flowing into the *eschara* and devoted to dead heroes and the chthonic deities, the cult of the hero stands in striking contrast to the Olympian aura with which the figure of "hero" is endowed by popular fantasy.

> It is the rarest exception (as in the case of Herakles) if he does not fall victim to death; he is always in contact with it, death belongs to his "shape" and the cult testifies to the last, destined turn of the hero life, for it is after all a cult of the dead.[265]

The hero is a figure not merely aerial and dazzling, and consciousness cannot afford to be either. The hero is inexorably centered and grounded in his earthly condition; maiden sacrifices made by him represent a transformation of the inner life, and the moral burdens of the entire process are his own to carry. The living hero strives ever onward, like the spirit-identified ego, but meets his chthonic counterpart in death. But the death of the hero is also a renewal in the indestructible life, for "Hades and Dionysos are the same thing." Kerényi thus quotes Heraclitus and goes on to describe a striking image of completion and of union with the feminine:

> Archaic gravestones from the neighborhood of Sparta let the secret out most clearly; recently a large find of clay tablets brings the same identity before our eyes. The god sits on a throne, with the same wine-cup, the *kantharos,* in his hand, or else a pomegranate, which he has offered to Persephone to eat; the Queen of the Underworld sits beside him. Other signs, the serpent, the dog, the horse, once also the youthful-looking head, offerings which little human figures are bringing the divine pair, all tell us unmistakably that his Hades and Dionysos in one person represent the "Heros."[266]

As defeating to the ego as this symbolic death may be, and however tormenting an approach to this actually gracious union may be, the imponderable unity of life and death asserts itself. It is a unity completely self-evident in the archetype of the feminine as mother and as anima; completely containing the vicissitudes of the battling ego and shadow; a unity transformed into psychic consciousness and given numinous and compelling meaning through the

CONIVNCTIO SIVE
Cottus.

O Luna durch meyn vmbgeben/vnd suſſe mynne/
Wirſtu ſchön/ſtarck/vnd gewaltig als ich byn.
O Sol/ du biſt vber alle liecht zu erkennen/
So bedarffſtu doch mein als der han der hennen.

Alchemical image of the *coniunctio*, union of masculine and feminine:
"O Moon, folded in my embrace/ Be you as strong as I, as fair of
face./ O Sun, brightest of all lights known to men/ And yet you need
me, as the cock the hen."—From *Rosarium philosophorum*, 1550.

sacrificial activity of the Self. Through impulse, containment, reflection and sacrifice a new spring bubbles forth, an illuminating vision
of an eternal continuing upon one's return from the ritual. Accordingly a final figure may conclude this search, like a constellation
flickering in the receding darkness:

> There is in the gateway the picture of an old man, white-haired,
> winged; he is pursuing a blue-colored woman who escapes. [The aged
> man is designated "light", and the woman "dark water."] The exact
> meaning of these mysterious paintings is probably lost forever; but it
> is scarcely rash to conjecture that the male figure is Eros. He pursues
> a woman; he is winged; that is like the ordinary Eros of common
> mythology. But this Eros is the Eros of the mysteries; not young but
> very ancient, and white-haired . . . eldest of all the gods.[267]

Notes

CW — *The Collected Works of C.G. Jung*

1. *Uniform Crime Reports*, 1973, 1980.
2. Susan Brownmiller, *Against Our Will*, p. 200.
3. Ibid., p. 201.
4. Richard Krafft-Ebing, *Psychopathia Sexualis*, p. 526.
5. Ibid.
6. Ibid., p. 5.
7. Diana E.H. Russell, *The Politics of Rape*, p. 260.
8. Brownmiller, p. 197.
9. Ibid., p. 199.
10. Ibid., p. 203.
11. Ibid., p. 191.
12. Ibid., p. 196.
13. Ibid.
14. Russell, p. 261.
15. Made available by Gary Schoener, Licensed Psychologist, Walk-In Counseling Center, Minneapolis.
16. Brownmiller, p. 8.
17. Ibid., p. 9.
18. Ibid., p. 11.
19. Ibid., p. 9.
20. Ibid.
21. Ibid., p. 21.
22. Ibid., p. 28.
23. Ibid., p. 31.
24. Ibid., p. 111.
25. Ibid., p. 113.
26. The Doors, "The End," Elektra Records, 1968.
27. Brownmiller, p. 228.
28. Ibid., p. 5.
29. *New York Times Book Review*, February 8, 1976, p. 41.
30. Robert Graves, *The Greek Myths*, vol. 1, p. 213.
31. Brownmiller, p. 313.
32. A. Nicholas Groth and H. Jean Birnbaum, *Men Who Rape*, p. 102.
33. Ibid.
34. Brownmiller, p. 229.

35. Duncan Chappell, Robley Geis and Gilbert Geis, eds., *Forcible Rape*, p. 30.

36. Helene Deutsch, *The Psychology of Women*. Despite her overriding concretism and orthodox Freudianism, Deutsch does recognize the deep androgynous nature of the psyche in passages throughout her work, e.g.: "But actually, absurd and paradoxical as it may sound, the psychic structure of woman does not consist exclusively in the 'eternal feminine.' It is true that femininity is her essential core, but around this core are layers and wrappings that are equally germane parts of the feminine soul and frequently valuable ones, indispensable for the preservation and development of this core. If we find the subsequent development of these elements, we find that they stem from the active, sometimes masculine components that . . . originate in the masculine part of the bisexual disposition" (p. 142).

37. Russell, p. 265.

38. Simone de Beauvoir, *The Second Sex*, p. 76.

39. Ibid. Important in regard to the "concept of value" is the attention given by Jung to judgments of value in his studies in word association and in discussions of the feeling function, as well as the urgent attention to ethical problems which characterizes Jung's writings as a whole.

40. Brownmiller, p. 192.

41. Ibid., p. 359.

42. Ann Wolbert Burgess and Lynda Lytle Holmstrom, *The Victim of Rape*, p. 233.

43. Chappell et al., p. 10.

44. Groth and Birnbaum, p. 124.

45. See Burgess and Holmstrom, p. 61: "Again and again we were given opinions and told jokes by businessmen, academicians, physicians, strict psychoanalysts, and others to the effect that you can't rape a woman unless she wants it or that the woman enjoys the rape experience."

46. Ibid., p. 44.

47. Ibid., pp. 44-45.

48. Ibid., p. 43.

49. Ibid., p. 60.

50. Russell, p. 226.

51. Ibid., p. 225.

52. Burgess and Holmstrom, p. 92.

53. Ibid., p. 93.

54. Ibid., p. 229.

55. Brownmiller, p. 22.

56. Burgess and Holmstrom, p. 86.

57. Sandra Sutherland and Donald J. Scherl, "Crisis Intervention with Victims of Rape," in Chappell et al., p. 334.

58. Ibid., 336.
59. Burgess and Holmstrom, p. 322.
60. Ibid., p. 318.
61. Ibid., pp. 322-323.
62. Ibid., p. 323.
63. Ibid., p. 159.
64. See *The Myth of Analysis* by James Hillman for a fascinating treatment of the masculine/feminine problem and the historical misogyny within medicine and psychology.
65. Krafft-Ebing, p. 81.
66. Ibid., p. 195.
67. Ibid., p. 215.
68. Ibid., p. 146.
69. Ibid., p. 209.
70. Ibid., p. 161.
71. Adolf Guggenbühl-Craig, *Marriage: Dead or Alive*, p. 74.
72. C.G. Jung, *Memories, Dreams, Reflections*, p. 150.
73. Betty Friedan, *The Feminine Mystique*, p. 366.
74. Guggenbühl-Craig, pp. 77-78.
75. Sigmund Freud, "Beyond the Pleasure Principle," *The Complete Psychological Works*, vol. 13, p. 57.
76. Jung makes specific mention of criminal rape only in *Psychiatric Studies*, CW 1. One instance is his allusion to the "attempt to simulate rape" by an hysterical woman in the essay "On the Psychology of So-Called Occult Phenomena" (par. 117); a second, the attempted rape on a patient in her youth in "On Manic Mood Disorders" (par. 197); and another, the charge of rape in the case history of a mental defective in "On Simulated Insanity" (par. 311). In addition there is the rather crude remark made by Jung in discussing the male reaction to the disagreeable effects of the animus in "The Syzygy: Anima and Animus," *Aion*, CW 9ii, which reads: "Often the man has the feeling—and he is not altogether wrong—that only seduction or a beating or rape would have the necessary power of pursuasion" (par. 29).

    In discussing the origin of fantasy material in *Symbols of Transformation*, CW 5, Jung also recognizes the archetypal nature of rape: "Quite apart from the fact that rape was a common occurrence in prehistoric times, it was also a popular theme of mythology in more civilized epochs. One has only to think of the rape of Persephone, of Deianira, Europa, and of the Sabine women. Nor should we forget that in many parts of the earth there are marriage customs existing today which recall the ancient marriage by capture.

    "One could give countless examples of this kind. They would all prove the same thing, namely that what, with us, is a subterranean fantasy was once open to the light of day" (pars. 34-35).

77. Freud, "The Economic Problem of Masochism," *Complete Works*, vol. 19, p. 161.

78. Ibid., p. 162.

79. Deutsch, p. 255.

80. Ibid., p. 190.

81. Ibid., p. 222.

82. Ibid., p. 223.

83. Erich Neumann, *Amor and Psyche.*

84. Marie-Louise von Franz, in *A Psychological Interpretation of The Golden Ass of Apuleius.*

85. De Beauvoir, p. 346.

86. Deutsch, p. 257.

87. Jung, "The Psychological Aspects of the Kore," *The Archetypes and the Collective Unconscious*, CW 9i, par. 311.

88. Deutsch, p. 148.

89. Patricia Berry, "The Demeter-Persephone Mythologem with Reference to Neurosis and Treatment."

90. Deutsch, p. 86.

91. Ibid., p. 87.

92. Karen Horney, *Feminine Psychology*, p. 43.

93. Berry, p. 5.

94. Brownmiller, p. 195 (my italics).

95. M.L. Cohen, R. Garfalo, R.B. Boucher, T. Seghorn, "The Psychology of Rapists," in Chappell et al., p. 295.

96. Ibid., p. 296.

97. Ibid., p. 297.

98. Ibid., pp. 297-298.

99. Brownmiller cites Guttmacher as a particularly sexist author in her own work *Against Our Will.*

100. Chappell et al., p. 296 (my italics).

101. Freud, *Three Essays on the Theory of Sexuality*, p. 25.

102. Groth and Birnbaum, p. 2.

103. Ibid., p. 28.

104. Ibid., p. 98 (my italics).

105. Ibid.

106. Ibid., p. 102.

107. Ibid., p. 28.

108. Ibid., p. 93.

109. Ibid., p. 90.

110. Ibid., p. 88.

111. Ibid., p. 89.

112. Ibid., p. 92.
113. Chappell et al., p. 313.
114. Jung, "Psychological Factors Determining Human Behavior," *The Structure and Dynamics of the Psyche*, CW 8, par. 243.
115. Groth and Birnbaum, p. 106.
116. Ibid., p. 6.
117. Jung, "Anima and Animus," *Two Essays on Analytical Psychology*, CW 7, par. 323.
118. Edward C. Whitmont, *The Symbolic Quest*, p. 223.
119. Chappell et al., p. 303.
120. Ibid.
121. Jung, *Symbols of Transformation*, CW 5, par. 508.
122. Reference is made to the blood motif in Jung's own "confrontation with the unconscious" as recorded in his autobiography, *Memories, Dreams, Reflections*, p. 175.
123. Horney, "The Dread of Women," p. 350.
124. James Hillman, *The Myth of Analysis*, p. 228.
125. De Beauvoir, pp. 199-200.
126. Hillman, *Myth of Analysis*, p. 246.
127. Wolfgang Lederer, *The Fear of Women*, p. 40.
128. Gary Fisher and Ephriam Rivlin, "Psychological Needs of Rapists," *British Journal of Criminology*, 11:182-85, 1971.
129. Horney, "The Dread of Women," p. 359.
130. Lederer, p. 46.
131. Ed Sanders, *The Family*, p. 142.
132. Ibid.
133. Ibid., p. 143.
134. Ibid., p. 152.
135. Ibid., p. 178.
136. Ibid., p. 192.
137. Lederer, p. 137.
138. Ibid., p. 141.
139. Ajit Mookerjee and Madhu Khanna, *The Tantric Way*, p. 85.
140. Mircea Eliade, *Patterns in Comparative Religion*, p. 38.
141. Ibid., p. 82.
142. Ibid., p. 93.
143. Erich Neumann, *The Origins and History of Consciousness*, p. 178 (my italics).
144. Ibid., p. 186.
145. R.H. Charles, *The Book of Enoch*, p. 112 (my italics).
146. Emma Jung, *Animus and Anima*, p. 3 (my italics).

147. Among the most famous—though by no means the first—witch-hunters, Heinrich Kramer and James Sprenger were the authors of the famous work, *Malleus Malificarum*, "The Witches' Hammer," a guide to inducing confessions through trial and torture of those suspected of witchcraft. Pope Innocence supported their efforts during the Inquisition in central Europe.

148. Jung, *Psychological Types*, CW 6, par. 86.

149. Ibid., par. 88.

150. Jung, CW 7, par. 256 (my italics).

151. Jung, CW 6, par. 819.

152. Ibid., par. 824.

153. Jung, "Paracelsus as a Spiritual Phenomenon," *Alchemical Studies*, CW 13, par. 176.

154. Jung, CW 9i, par. 178.

155. Groth and Birnbaum, p. 106.

156. Jung, CW 9i, par. 167.

157. Horney, "The Dread of Women," p. 353 (my italics).

158. De Beauvoir, p. 418 (my italics).

159. James Hillman, *The Dream and the Underworld*, p. 57.

160. Medard Boss, *Meaning and Content of Sexual Perversions*, pp. 91-92 (my italics).

161. Ibid., p. 96.

162. Krafft-Ebing, p. 109.

163. Groth and Birnbaum, p. 45.

164. Ibid., p. 47.

165. Ibid.

166. Ibid., p. 44.

167. Ibid., p. 48.

168. Brownmiller, p. 367.

169. Ibid., p. 368.

170. De Beauvoir, p. 173.

171. Ibid., pp. 175-176.

172. Jung, CW 7, par. 301.

173. Ibid., par. 314.

174. Jung, CW 5, par. 678.

175. Jung, CW 9i, par. 381.

176. Horney, "The Dread of Women," p. 349.

177. Groth and Birnbaum, p. 36.

178. Jung, CW 9i, par. 356.

179. Ibid., par. 355.

180. Hillman, *The Dream and the Underworld*, p. 145.

181. Jung, CW 9i, par. 57.

182. Marquis de Sade, *The One Hundred and Twenty Days of Sodom*, p. 266.

183. Jung, CW 9i, par. 61.

184. See Hillman's *Myth of Analysis* and his "Anima," (I and II).

185. Hillman, "Anima" (I), *Spring 1973*, p. 103.

186. Eldridge Cleaver, *Soul On Ice*, p. 6.

187. Ibid., p. 13.

188. Ibid., p. 14.

189. Ibid.

190. John A. Oliver, *Eldridge Cleaver Reborn*, pp. 216-227.

191. Apuleius, *The Golden Ass*, p. 272.

192. Jung, CW 6, par. 381.

193. Ibid.

194. Ibid., pars. 383-385.

195. Ibid., par. 396.

196. Norman Cohn, *Europe's Inner Demons*, p. 87.

197. Jung, CW 6, par. 399.

198. Burgess and Holmstrom, p. 177.

199. R.E.L. Masters, *Eros and Evil*, p. 6.

200. Ibid., p. 65.

201. Ibid., p. 66.

202. Friedrich Schwenn, *Die Menschenopfer bei den Griechen und Römer*, p. 30.

203. De Beauvoir, p. 196.

204. Ibid., pp. 202-203 (my italics).

205. Ibid., p. 202.

206. Jane Harrison, *Prolegomena to the Study of Greek Religion*, p. 309.

207. Ibid., p. 302.

208. Ibid., p. 303.

209. A. Nicholas Groth, *American Journal of Psychiatry*, 137:806-10, July, 1980.

210. Brownmiller, p. 288.

211. Ibid., p. 290.

212. Jean Genet, *The Miracle of the Rose*, p. 112.

213. Ibid., p. 93.

214. See John Weir Perry's *The Far Side of Madness* for a study of the transformative possibilities of psychosis.

215. Wallis Budge, *The Gods of the Egyptians*, vol. 2, plate 40.

216. Otto Fenichel, *The Psychoanalytic Theory of Neurosis*, p. 427.

217. Ibid., p. 428.

218.   Ibid., p. 429.
219.   Ibid., p. 430 (first italics mine).
220.   Ibid., p. 432.
221.   John Layard, "Homoeroticism in Primitive Society as a Function of the Self," *Journal of Analytical Psychology*, 4,2, 1959, p. 251.
222.   Ibid., p. 254.
223.   Ibid.
224.   Ibid., p. 251.
225.   St. Bernard of Clairvaux, sermon 29:11 (in Santos, p. 54).
226.   Hillman, *Myth of Analysis*, p. 64.
227.   Jung, CW 5, par. 574.
228.   Ibid., par. 571.
229.   Ibid., par. 572.
230.   Ibid., par. 575 (my italics).
231.   James George Frazer, *The Golden Bough*, p. 169.
232.   Ibid., p. 168.
233.   Fray Diego Duran, *The Book of Gods and Rites and the Ancient Calendar*, p. 222.
234.   Ibid., pp. 222-223.
235.   Ibid., p. 223.
236.   Ibid., p. 226.
237.   D.H. Lawrence, "The Woman Who Rode Away," *The Complete Short Stories of D.H. Lawrence*, vol. II, p. 581.
238.   See Jung and Kerényi on the archetype of the divine child, in *Essays on a Science of Mythology*.
239.   Harrison, p. 197.
240.   Ibid.
241.   Jung, "Transformation Symbolism in the Mass," *Psychology and Religion*, CW 11, par. 389.
242.   Ibid., par. 405.
243.   Neumann, *Origins*, p. 78.
244.   John Layard, "The Identification with the Sacrificial Animal," p. 98.
245.   Ibid., p. 342.
246.   Ibid., p. 355.
247.   Jung, CW 11, par. 398.
248.   Ibid., par. 400.
249.   Jung, CW 5, par. 671.
250.   Harrison, p. 58.
251.   Ibid., pp. 61-62.
252.   Ibid., p. 63.
253.   Ibid., p. 64.

254.   Ibid., p. 65.
255.   C. Kerényi, *The Heroes of the Greeks*, p. 37.
256.   Ibid., p. 206.
257.   Ibid.
258.   Neumann, *Amor and Psyche*, p. 67.
259.   Kerényi, *Heroes*, p. 238.
260.   Ibid., p. 332.
261.   Ibid., p. 333.
262.   Jung, CW 5, par. 669.
263.   Kerényi, *Heroes*, p. 13.
264.   Ibid.
265.   Ibid., p. 14.
266.   Ibid., p. 16.
267.   Harrison, p. 644. This image in a ritual bridal chamber is described by an anonymous Greek author in a work called *Philosophoumena*, discussed by Harrison. The chamber was probably part of a telesterion at Phyla and may have been used in initiation rituals related to Orphism.

Glossary of Jungian Terms

Anima (Latin, "soul"). The unconscious, feminine side of a man's personality. She is personified in dreams by images of women ranging from prostitute and seductress to spiritual guide (Wisdom). She is the eros principle, hence a man's anima development is reflected in how he relates to women. Identification with the anima can appear as moodiness, effeminacy, and oversensitivity. Jung calls the anima *the archetype of life itself.*

Animus (Latin, "spirit"). The unconscious, masculine side of a woman's personality. He personifies the logos principle. Identification with the animus can cause a woman to become rigid, opinionated, and argumentative. More positively, he is the inner man who acts as a bridge between the woman's ego and her own creative resources in the unconscious.

Archetypes. Irrepresentable in themselves, but their effects appear in consciousness as the archetypal images and ideas. These are universal patterns or motifs which come from the collective unconscious and are the basic content of religions, mythologies, legends, and fairytales. They emerge in individuals through dreams and visions.

Association. A spontaneous flow of interconnected thoughts and images around a specific idea, determined by unconscious connections.

Complex. An emotionally charged group of ideas or images. At the "center" of a complex is an archetype or archetypal image.

Constellate. Whenever there is a strong emotional reaction to a person or a situation, a complex has been constellated (activated).

Ego. The central complex in the field of consciousness. A strong ego can relate objectively to activated contents of the unconscious (i.e., other complexes), rather than identifying with them, which appears as a state of possession.

Feeling. One of the four psychic functions. It is a rational function which evaluates the worth of relationships and situations. Feeling must be distinguished from emotion, which is due to an activated complex.

Individuation. The conscious realization of one's unique psychological reality, including both strengths and limitations. It leads to the experience of the Self as the regulating center of the psyche.

Inflation. A state in which one has an unrealistically high or low (negative inflation) sense of identity. It indicates a regression of consciousness into unconsciousness, which typically happens when the ego takes too many unconscious contents upon itself and loses the faculty of discrimination.

Intuition. One of the four psychic functions. It is the irrational function which tells us the possibilities inherent in the present. In contrast to sensation (the function which perceives immediate reality through the physical senses) intuition perceives via the unconscious, e.g., flashes of insight of unknown origin.

147

Participation mystique. A term derived from the anthropologist Lévy-Bruhl, denoting a primitive, psychological connection with objects, or between persons, resulting in a strong unconscious bond.

Persona (Latin, "actor's mask"). One's social role, derived from the expectations of society and early training. A strong ego relates to the outside world through a flexible persona; identification with a specific persona (doctor, scholar, artist, etc.) inhibits psychological development.

Projection. The process whereby an unconscious quality or characteristic of one's own is perceived and reacted to in an outer object or person. Projection of the anima or animus onto a real women or man is experienced as falling in love. Frustrated expectations indicate the need to withdraw projections, in order to relate to the reality of other people.

Puer aeternus (Latin, "eternal youth"). Indicates a certain type of man who remains too long in adolescent psychology, generally associated with a strong unconscious attachment to the mother (actual or symbolic). Positive traits are spontaneity and openness to change. His female counterpart is the **puella,** an "eternal girl" with a corresponding attachment to the father-world.

Self. The archetype of wholeness and the regulating center of the personality. It is experienced as a transpersonal power which transcends the ego, e.g., God.

Senex (Latin, "old man"). Associated with attitudes that come with advancing age. Negatively, this can mean cynicism, rigidity and extreme conservatism; positive traits are responsibility, orderliness and self-discipline. A well-balanced personality functions appropriately within the puer-senex polarity.

Shadow. An unconscious part of the personality characterized by traits and attitudes, whether negative or positive, which the conscious ego tends to reject or ignore. It is personified in dreams by persons of the same sex as the dreamer. Consciously assimilating one's shadow usually results in an increase of energy.

Symbol. The best possible expression for something essentially unknown. Symbolic thinking is non-linear, right-brain oriented; it is complementary to logical, linear, left-brain thinking.

Transcendent function. The reconciling "third" which emerges from the unconscious (in the form of a symbol or a new attitude) after the conflicting opposites have been consciously differentiated, and the tension between them held.

Transference and countertransference. Particular cases of projection, commonly used to describe the unconscious, emotional bonds that arise between two persons in an analytic or therapeutic relationship.

Uroboros. The mythical snake or dragon that eats its own tail. It is a symbol both for individuation as a self-contained, circular process, and for narcissistic self-absorption.

Bibliography

Amir, Menachem. *Patterns in Forcible Rape.* University of Chicago Press, Chicago, 1971.

Apuleius. *The Golden Ass.* Trans. Harold Berman. Privately printed, 1930.

Berry, Patricia. "The Demeter-Persephone Mythologem with Reference to Neurosis and Treatment." Diploma Thesis. C.G. Jung Institute, Zurich, 1975.

Boss, Medard. *Meaning and Content of Sexual Perversions.* Grune and Stratton, New York, 1949.

Brownmiller, Susan. *Against Our Will: Men, Women and Rape.* Bantam (Simon and Schuster), New York, 1975.

Budge, Wallis. *The Gods of the Egyptians,* vol. 2. Dover Publications, New York, 1969.

Burgess, Ann Wolbert, and Lynda Lytle Holmstrom. *The Victim of Rape: Institutional Reactions.* John Wiley and Sons, New York, 1978.

Chappell, Duncan, Robley Geis and Gilbert Geis, Eds. *Forcible Rape: The Crime, the Victim and the Offender.* Columbia University Press, New York, 1977.

Charles, R.H. *The Book of Enoch,* Clarendon Press, Oxford, 1893.

Cleaver, Eldridge. *Soul on Ice.* Dell Publishing Co., New York, 1968.

Cohn, Norman. *Europe's Inner Demons: An Inquiry Inspired by the Great Witchhunt.* Chatto and Heinemann for Sussex University Press, 1975.

De Beauvoir, Simone. *The Second Sex.* Penguin Books, London, 1979.

De Sade, Marquis. *The One Hundred and Twenty Days of Sodom.* Grove Press, New York, 1967.

Deutsch, Helene. *The Psychology of Women,* vol. 1. Grune and Stratton, New York, 1944.

Duran, Fray Diego. *The Book of Gods and Rites and the Ancient Calendar.* University of Oklahoma Press, Norma, 1975.

Eliade, Mircea. *Patterns in Comparative Religion.* Sheed and Ward, London, 1976.

Fenichel, Otto. *The Psychoanalytic Theory of Neurosis.* W.W. Norton and Co., New York, 1945.

Frazer, James George. *The Golden Bough.* Macmillan Publishing Co., New York, 1974.

Freud, Sigmund. *The Complete Psychological Works of Sigmund Freud,* vols. XVIII, XIX. Ed. James Strachey. The Hogarth Press and the Institute of Psychoanalysis, London, 1978.

———. *Three Essays on the Theory of Sexuality.* Ed. James Strachey. Basic Books, New York, 1975.

Friedan, Betty. *The Feminine Mystique.* Dell Publishing Co., New York, 1963.

Genet, Jean. *The Miracle of the Rose.* Penguin Books, London, 1965.

Giger, Hans Rudi. *Necronomicon.* Sphinx Verlag, Basel, 1978.

Graves, Robert. *The Greek Myths.* George Braziller, New York, 1957.

Groth, A. Nicholas, and H. Jean Birnbaum. *Men Who Rape.* Plenum Press, New York, 1980.

Guggenbühl-Craig, Adolf. *Marriage: Dead or Alive.* Spring Publications, Zurich, 1976.

Harrison, Jane. *Prolegomena to the Study of Greek Religion.* Merlin Press, London, 1980.

Hillman, James. "Anima" (I and II). *Spring 1973, 1974.* Spring Publications, Zurich.

——— . *The Dream and the Underworld.* Harper and Row, New York, 1979.

——— . *The Myth of Analysis.* Northwestern University Press, Evanston, 1972.

——— . *Pan and the Nightmare.* Spring Publications, Zurich, 1972.

Horney, Karen. "The Dread of Women." *International Journal of Psychoanalysis,* XIII, 1932.

——— . *Feminine Psychology.* W.W. Norton and Co., New York, 1973.

Jung, C.G. *The Collected Works* (Bollingen Series XX). 20 vols. Trans. R.F.C. Hull. Ed. H. Read, M. Fordham, G. Adler, Wm. McGuire. Princeton University Press, Princeton, 1953-1979.

——— . *Memories, Dreams, Reflections.* Ed. Aniela Jaffe, Random House, New York, 1961.

——— , and C. Kerényi. *Essays on a Science of Mythology.* Harper and Row, New York, 1949.

Jung, Emma. *Animus and Anima.* Spring Publications, Zurich, 1978.

Kerényi, C. *The Gods of the Greeks.* Thames and Hudson, London, 1979.

——— . *The Heroes of the Greeks.* Thames and Hudson, London, 1978.

Krafft-Ebing, Richard. *Psychopathia Sexualis.* Medical Arts Agency, New York, 1900.

Lawrence, D.H. *The Complete Short Stories of D.H. Lawrence,* vol. II. Heinemann, London, 1968.

Layard, John. "Homoeroticism in Primitive Society as a Function of the Self." *Journal of Analytical Psychology,* 4,2, 1959.

——— . "The Identification with the Sacrificial Animal." *Eranos Jahrbuch,* Band XXIV, Rhein Verlang, Zurich, 1955.

Lederer, Wolfgang. *The Fear of Women.* Harcourt, Brace, Jovanovich, New York, 1968.

Lopez-Pedraza, Raphael. *Hermes and His Children.* Spring Publications, Zurich, 1977.

Masters, R.E.L. *Eros and Evil: The Sexual Psychopathology of Witchcraft.* Julian Press, New York, 1962.

Medea, Andra, Thompson, Katherine. *Against Rape.* Farrar, Straus and Giroux, New York, 1974.

Mookerjee, Ajit, and Madhu Khanna. *The Tantric Way: Art, Science, Ritual.* Thames and Hudson, London, 1977.

Neumann, Erich. *Amor and Psyche, The Psychological Development of the Feminine* (Bollingen Series LIV). Princeton University Press, Princeton, 1971.

―――. *The Origins and History of Consciousness* (Bollingen Series XLII). Princeton University Press, Princeton, 1973.

Oliver, John A. *Eldridge Cleaver Reborn.* Logos International, Plainfield, 1977.

Perry, John Weir. *The Far Side of Madness.* Prentice Hall, Englewood Cliffs, 1974.

Plato, *Symposium,* Penguin Books, London, 1980.

Russell, Diana E.H. *The Politics of Rape: The Victim's Perspective.* Stein and Day, New York, 1974.

Sanders, Ed. *The Family.* Avon Books, New York, 1972.

Santos, Gregory John. "Psychological Parallels Between C.G. Jung and St. Bernard's Sermons on the Song of Songs." Diploma Thesis. C.G. Jung Institute, Zurich, 1978.

Schwenn, Friedrich. *Die Menschenopfer bei den Griechen und Römern.* Verlag Alfred Töpelmann, Münster, 1915.

Uniform Crime Reports. United States Government Publication, 1981.

Von Franz, Marie-Louise. *A Psychological Interpretation of the Golden Ass of Apuleius.* Spring Publications, Zurich, 1970.

―――. *Alchemy: An Introduction to the Symbolism and the Psychology.* Inner City Books, Toronto, 1980.

Whitmont, Edward C. *The Symbolic Quest.* Harper and Row, New York, 1969.

Index

Studies in Jungian Psychology by Jungian Analysts

LIMITED EDITION PAPERBACKS

1. The Secret Raven: Conflict and Transformation.
Daryl Sharp (Toronto). ISBN 0-919123-00-7. 128 pages. $10/£5.

The best-selling depth analysis of artistic despair. Sympathetic, perceptive and concise. Focuses on the life of the writer Franz Kafka, but the psychology is relevant to anyone who has experienced a conflict between instinctual demands and the spiritual life, or between love and sex. (Previous knowledge of Kafka is not necessary.) Illustrated. Bibliography. Index.

2. The Psychological Meaning of Redemption Motifs in Fairytales.
Marie-Louise von Franz (Zurich). ISBN 0-919123-01-5. 128 pages. $10/£5.

A unique account of the significance of fairytales for an understanding of the process of individuation, especially in terms of integrating animal nature and human nature. Particularly helpful for its symbolic, nonlinear approach to the meaning of typical dream motifs (bathing, beating, clothes, animals, etc.), and its clear description of complexes and projection. Index.

3. On Divination and Synchronicity: The Psychology of Meaningful Chance.
Marie-Louise von Franz (Zurich). ISBN 0-919123-02-3. 128 pages. $10/£5.

A penetrating study of the meaning of the irrational. Examines time, number, and methods of divining fate such as the I Ching, astrology, Tarot, palmistry, random patterns, etc. Explains and illustrates Jung's ideas on archetypes, projection, psychic energy and synchronicity, contrasting Western scientific attitudes with those of the Chinese and so-called primitives. Illustrated. Index.

4. The Owl Was a Baker's Daughter: Obesity, Anorexia Nervosa, and the Repressed Feminine.
Marion Woodman (Toronto). ISBN 0-919123-03-1. 144 pages. $10/£5.

A pioneer work in feminine psychology, with particular attention to the body as mirror of the psyche in eating disorders and weight disturbances. Explores the personal and cultural loss—and potential rediscovery—of the feminine principle, through Jung's Association Experiment, case studies, dreams, Christianity and mythology. Illustrated. Glossary. Bibliography. Index.

5. Alchemy: An Introduction to the Symbolism and the Psychology.
Marie-Louise von Franz (Zurich). ISBN 0-919123-04-X. 288 pages. $16/£8.

A lucid and practical guide to what the alchemists were really looking for—emotional balance and wholeness. Completely demystifies the subject. An important work, invaluable for an understanding of images and motifs in modern dreams and drawings, and indispensable for anyone interested in relationships and communication between the sexes. 84 Illustrations. Index.

6. Descent to the Goddess: A Way of Initiation for Women.
Sylvia Brinton Perera (New York). ISBN 0-919123-05-8. 112 pages. $10/£5.

A timely and provocative study of women's freedom and the need for an inner, female authority in a masculine-oriented society. Based on the Sumerian goddess Inanna-Ishtar's journey to the underworld, her transformation through contact with her dark "sister" Ereshkigal, and her return. Rich in insights from dreams, mythology and analysis. Glossary. Bibliography. Index.

7. C.G. Jung and Paul Tillich: The Psyche as Sacrament.
John P. Dourley (Ottawa). ISBN 0-919123-06-6. 128 pages. $10/£5.

An illuminating, comparative study showing with great clarity that in the depths of the soul the psychological task and the religious task are one. With a dual perspective, the author—Jungian analyst and Catholic priest—examines the deeper meaning, for Christian and non-Christian alike, of God, Christ, the Spirit, the Trinity, morality and much else. Glossary. Index.

Please see reverse

8. Border Crossings: A Psychological Perspective on Carlos Castaneda's Path of Knowledge.
Donald Lee Williams (Boulder). ISBN 0-919123-07-4. 160 pages. $12/£6.

The first thorough psychological examination of the popular don Juan novels. Using dreams, fairytales, and mythic and cultural parallels, the author brings Castaneda's spiritual journey down to earth, in terms of everyone's search for self-realization. Demonstrates that our experience of the unconscious, rather than a problem to be solved, is an invitation to live more fully. Special attention to the psychology of women, Native American images and the analytic process. (Familiarity with the novels is not necessary.) Glossary. Bibliography. Index.

9. Narcissism and Character Transformation: Psychology of Narcissistic Character Disorders.
Nathan Schwartz-Salant (New York). ISBN 0-919123-08-2. 192 pages. $13/£7.

An incisive and comprehensive analysis of narcissism: what it looks like, what it means and how to deal with it. Through extensive case material and versions of the Narcissus myth, the author shows how an understanding of the archetypal patterns that underlie the individual, clinical symptoms of narcissism can point the way to a healthy restructuring of the personality. Draws upon a variety of psychoanalytic points of view (Jungian, Freudian, Kohutian, Kleinian, etc.). Special emphasis on body awareness. Illustrated. Glossary. Bibliography. Index.

10. Rape and Ritual: A Psychological Study.
Bradley A. Te Paske (Minneapolis). ISBN 0-919123-09-0. 160 pages. $12/£6.

An absorbing combination of theory, clinical material, dreams and mythology, penetrating far beyond the actual deed to the impersonal, archetypal background of sexual assault. Special attention to male ambivalence, the psychological significance of rape dreams and fantasies, and the role of sacrifice in the individuation process. Illustrated. Glossary. Bibliography. Index.

11. Alcoholism and Women: The Background and the Psychology.
Jan Bauer (Zurich). ISBN 0-919123-10-4. 144 pages. $12/£6.

A major contribution to an understanding of alcoholism, particularly in women. Examines social attitudes, compares and contrasts medical and psychological models, illustrates the relative merits of Alcoholics Anonymous and individual therapy, and presents new ways of looking at the problem based on case material, dreams and archetypal patterns. Bibliography. Index.

12. Addiction to Perfection: The Still Unravished Bride.
Marion Woodman (Toronto). ISBN 0-919123-11-2. 160 pages. $12/£6.

A powerful and authoritative look at the psychology and attitudes of modern woman, expanding on the themes introduced by the author in *The Owl Was a Baker's Daughter*. Explores the nature of the feminine through case material, dreams and mythology, in food rituals, rape symbolism, perfectionism, imagery in the body, sexuality and creativity. Illustrated. Bibliography. Index.